AF472288

Guy Ben-Ari
DEMOCRACY SOUP

Drawings by Guy Ben-Ari
Ink on vellum, 2016, 8 x 5 inches each
Text by Eric Sutphin
Design by Suzie Apostolides

Thanks to Gregory Amenoff, Suzie Apostolides, Boaz Arad, Garet Edwards, Ido Bar El, Tae In Ahn, Lior Modan, Mark Joshua Epstein, Jonathan Durham, Netta Reichenberg, Judith Selkowitz, Oded Shatil, Shelly Silver, Jennifer Wade, Amy Zion and Calder Zwicky.

Special thanks to Leah Wolff.

www.DemocracySoup.com

First edition, 2016
Published by Meta Meta Meta, LLC
47 Hall Street, Suite B6
Brooklyn, New York 11205
www.metametameta.org

ISBN 978-1-365-14951-1

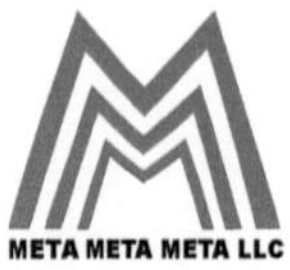

Guy Ben-Ari

DEMOCRACY SOUP

Eric Sutphin

DEMOCRACY SOUP

If the shrill timbre of a radio broadcast could be softened to a din, we might have a better chance at hearing / discerning its contents or non-content. Instead, tinny voices pierce through and puncture our daily rituals. *Drawing as antidote.* The ink is placed upon the vellum, thinned to varying consistencies; undulating, swelling, spreading out across an undefined expanse (Time). It's the raw material of a life, coalescing into a semblance, unformed, as it slowly, imperceptibly moves and populates an emptiness just beyond my purview — a mass around which this inchoate stuff begins to bend, eventually encasing it, dissolving it into mass, volume.

The drawings in this book are organized into five "types": portraits, hand gestures, abstractions, White House imagery and electoral maps. *Democracy Soup* is a funny title for a book of drawings - tongue in cheek - implying the brothy mess that is contemporary politics. But Guy Ben-Ari sidesteps generalized or reactionary commentary (the type of which invariably floods news-feeds during an election year). His drawings are formally delightful; liquidy washes of ink gather around visages, podiums, still lifes, maps and abstract forms. His approach to the subject seems idiosyncratic: he treats the hallowed with a nonchalant frankness, neither minimizing nor celebrating his subject(s). The more staged, prepared and stiff the image the better, it gives Ben-Ari more liberty to untangle it with his brush and inkpot. The images are cast into grisaille. Drawing as a discursive tool, a thinking tool, an apparatus, a container. Iris Murdoch: *Inspiration comes to us from out of the dark of non-being as a reward for loving attention.*[1]

Stage

May 11, 2016: On my way to buffalo, sitting in a small passenger jet, I wonder:

How is my non-regional dialect?

Who are you voting for?

Is there a viable third-party candidate?

Are you an anti-feminist if you don't vote for Hillary Clinton?

Are you ill-informed/too idealist/a socialist if you support Bernie Sanders?

Is Trump evil?

Are debates and speeches aesthetic experiences?

When we use the word "rhetoric" we often use it as a pejorative but rhetoric can be measured discourse, too.

---

[1] Iris Murdoch, *Metaphysics as a Guide to Morals* (London: Penguin Books, 1993), 505.

Proscenium

When I return home I flip open Roland Barthes' Mythologies. For any inquiry one might have regarding politics, wrestling, mothers, photography (or any combination of these things) R.B. is a good starting point. Barthes says: *Inasmuch as photography is an ellipse of language and condensation of an 'ineffable' social whole, it constitutes an anti-intellectual weapon and tends to spirit away 'politics' (that is to say a body of problems and solutions) to the advantage of a 'manner of being', a socio-moral status.*[2]

When we talk about a candidate's "electability" are we speaking to his or her policies or are we really talking about the way they look? What does it mean to look "presidential"? As one for the most photographed figures of all time, the President of the United States of America ought to be comfortable in front of a camera.

On April 9, 2016, I visited Guy Ben-Ari at his studio where he was working on Democracy Soup. Here is an excerpt of our conversation:

ES: As you are working on these drawings, are you scanning the news or the Internet for images?

GBA: Most of the images that I find come from Google searches of television broadcasts of network news, while some are from image banks, debates, and official White House correspondence. I'm looking for the formulated, manufactured images that were carefully crafted and produced, which I then crop or focus on details.

ES: So you are seeking out staged imagery rather than candid images?

GBA: I prefer images where the ideology is already embedded in them. I can find a small moment in those frames that might reveal something, like minor slips, a moment when the candidate accidently swears, a facial expression, or the way they stand on stage. For the majority of the time, they are clearly performing.

ES: Like when Carson and Trump messed up their entrance?

GBA: Exactly. Within that brief moment their interaction becomes honest or sincere. Another example would be the debate between Clinton and Bush in 1992. The candidates were getting questions from the audience, and as Bush was being asked a question he checked his watch. He came off as disinterested and distant, and was fiercely criticized later for what that minor gesture signified. In that brief moment of nonverbal communication he gave away a lot.

---

[2] Roland Barthes, "Photography and Electoral Appeal", *Mythologies* (New York: Farrar, Straus and Giroux: 1972), 91.

ES: In those debates, since everything is so planned and scripted, those small incidental moments become the stand-ins for real content, real meaning.

GBA: That is why I like the moment when the candidates are on stage but the debate has not started yet. For example, when they are standing for the national anthem. I like those before and after moments.

ES: Drawing is the most fundamental, elemental aspect of art making -- are you using this elementary medium to dismantle political phenomena?

GBA: Yes, I think of drawing as the most direct way to mediate between the body, the action itself and the subject. To me, the original images are so thoroughly prepared and produced by someone else, and drawing allows me to break the images apart in an intimate way. I could do that in a painting too, but with drawing I can think about the structure more closely and in a different way.

ES: You are working against the material, the source material in these drawings. Your paintings become more of an approximation to the source. The scale too. The paintings seem more like a simulation of the material whereas one can see the drawings as a parsing of it. Of course, painting can be used as a critical tool as well...so maybe that's the function of the drawings, as way toward a critical painting?

GBA: Because the paintings are more about simulation, I wanted the images in the drawings to fall apart, have them deconstruct in a way. The image breaks apart and can be approached critically in a way that is more elemental. I found that missing in the paintings, where I was trying to get to the same effect. Through the dissolution of the original image, the paintings could develop into this abstract mess. For example, I could combine imagery from two different presidential debates, making the figurative elements less intelligible, but the content would still be there.

ES: I wonder if these drawings are even political. Is it possible to use political material and end up with a non-political work. They are not apolitical, but they're not directional. You are not taking a position in terms of "picking a side". That's not evident here. It seems you're thinking more specifically about the politics of imagery and symbols.

GBA: Taking a non-political position, trying to show some balance, part of that is about delaying the easy read. I think it inherently becomes political just based on the community I am a part of... since I was born in Israel and now live here in New York.

ES: You mean the art community?

GBA: Yes, the art community as well, but perhaps even more for being an artist that

was born in Israel and chose to move to the United States. Perhaps this doesn't really allow for an entirely neutralized reading of this work.

ES: Had you done these drawings six months or a year ago, the figures (candidates) would have had a different portent than they do today. But as we barrel toward Election Day, it must become more difficult to represent the front-runner's image - every day, every second, every minute - becomes more loaded.

GBA: That's part of what drove me to start working with images of Romney, along with candidates from 2012 and earlier. Because those images have already been processed, so they are not changing as much. It's more about the visual content that we have absorbed, it's already been absorbed, it's a part of the game: this person needs to look presidential and this is how it's done... I like how, for example, when a sitting president debates a candidate, once the two step onto the same stage, they are instantly presented as equal simply by way of the theater around them, no matter who the opponent is.

ES: You've omitted a lot of the text in these drawings, I imagine that in the original images there would have been logos, signs, banners, more text elements. We see it occasionally, but can you talk about your decision to remove most of the text?

GBA: Most of the text would be in the "debate background" drawings, on a banner reading 'Republican Presidential Debate', or something like that. To include that in the drawings made them feel a little too specific. Sometimes I like including the television networks' logos, but otherwise the text makes it feel too direct of a commentary, rather than a response to the imagery. Once there's text, you tend to hold onto it and stop looking at the drawing, and the drawing tends to become flattened.

ES: Seeing stops and reading begins.

Guy Ben-Ari

DEMOCRACY SOUP

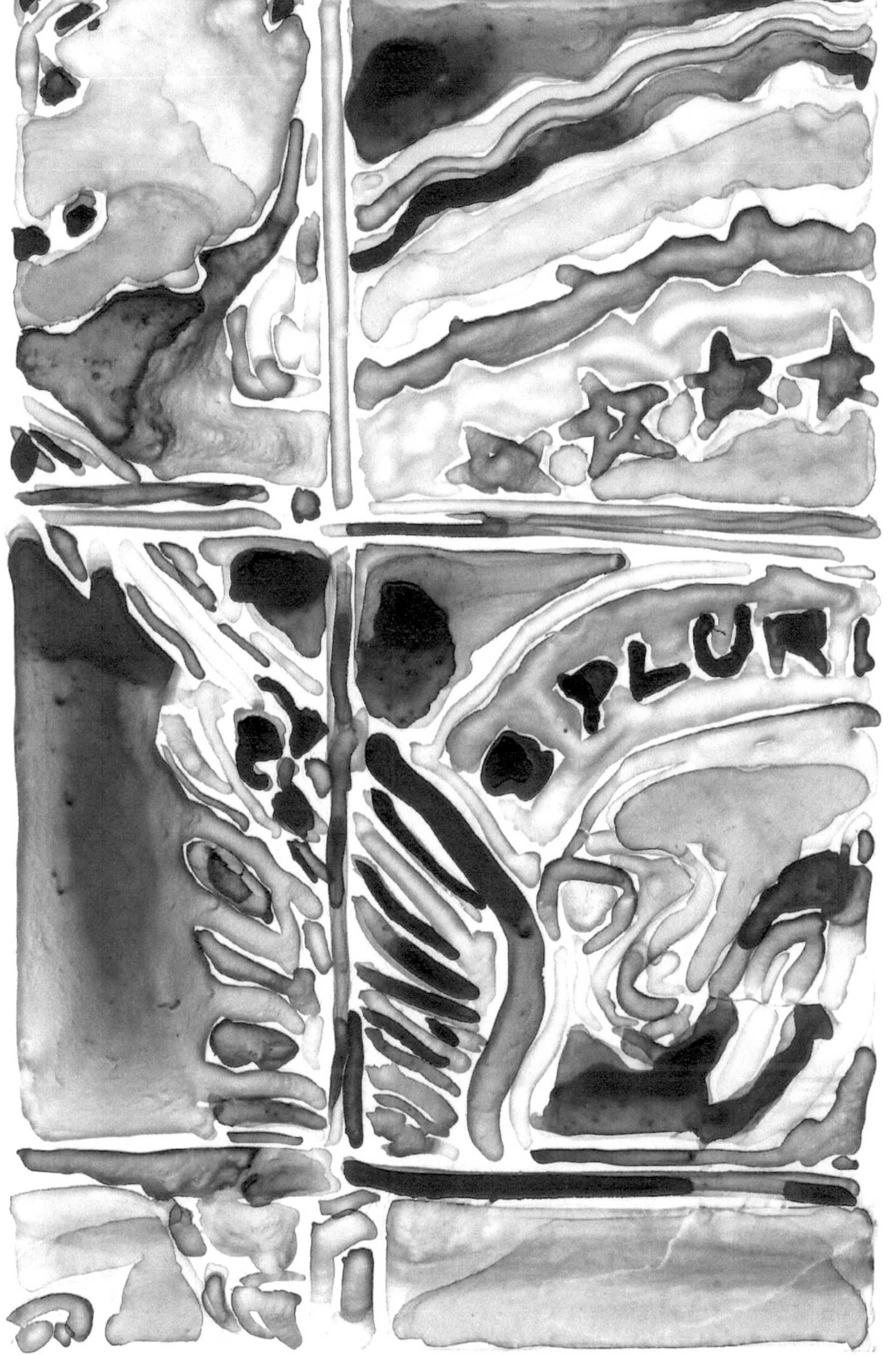
PLURI

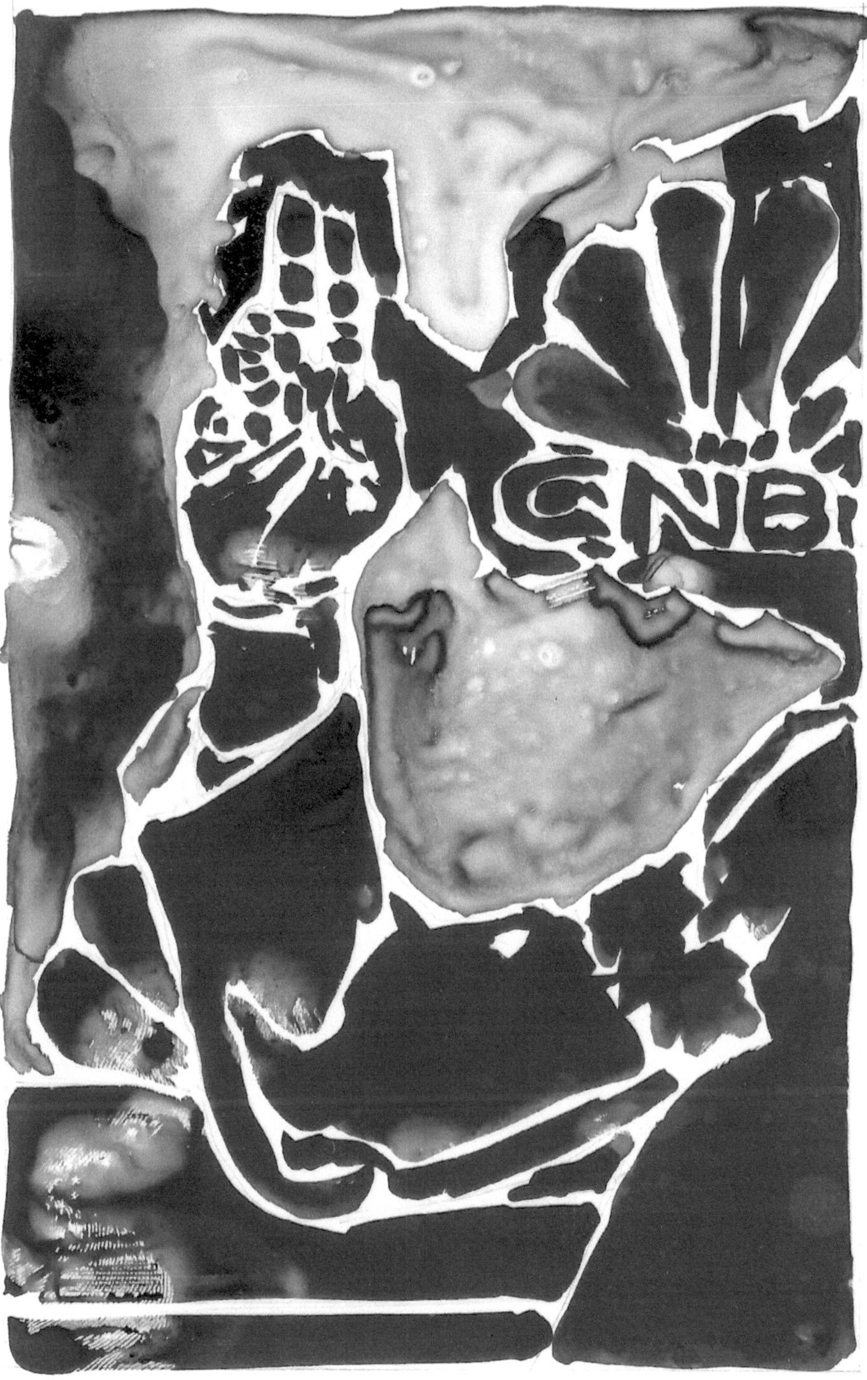

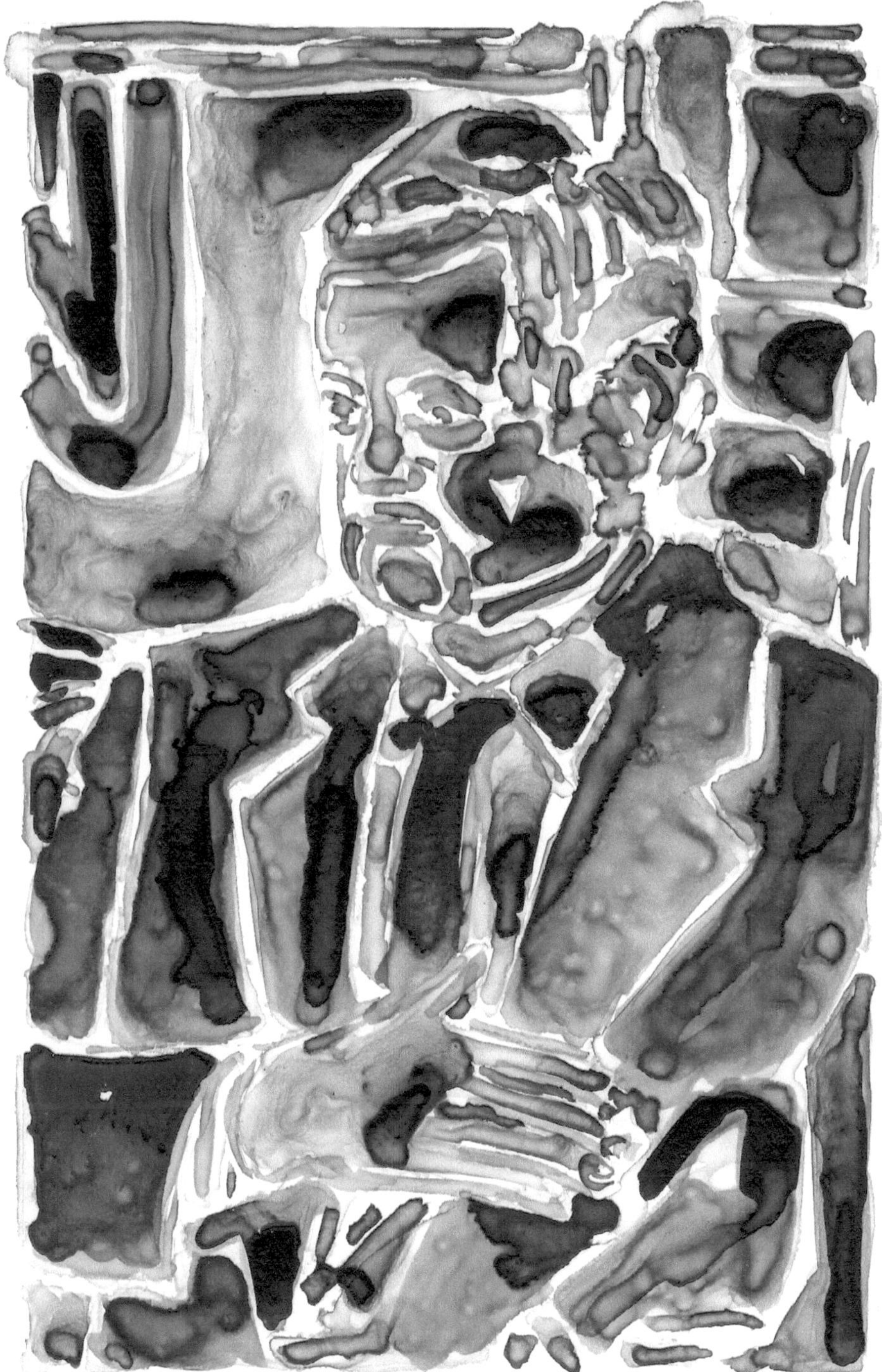

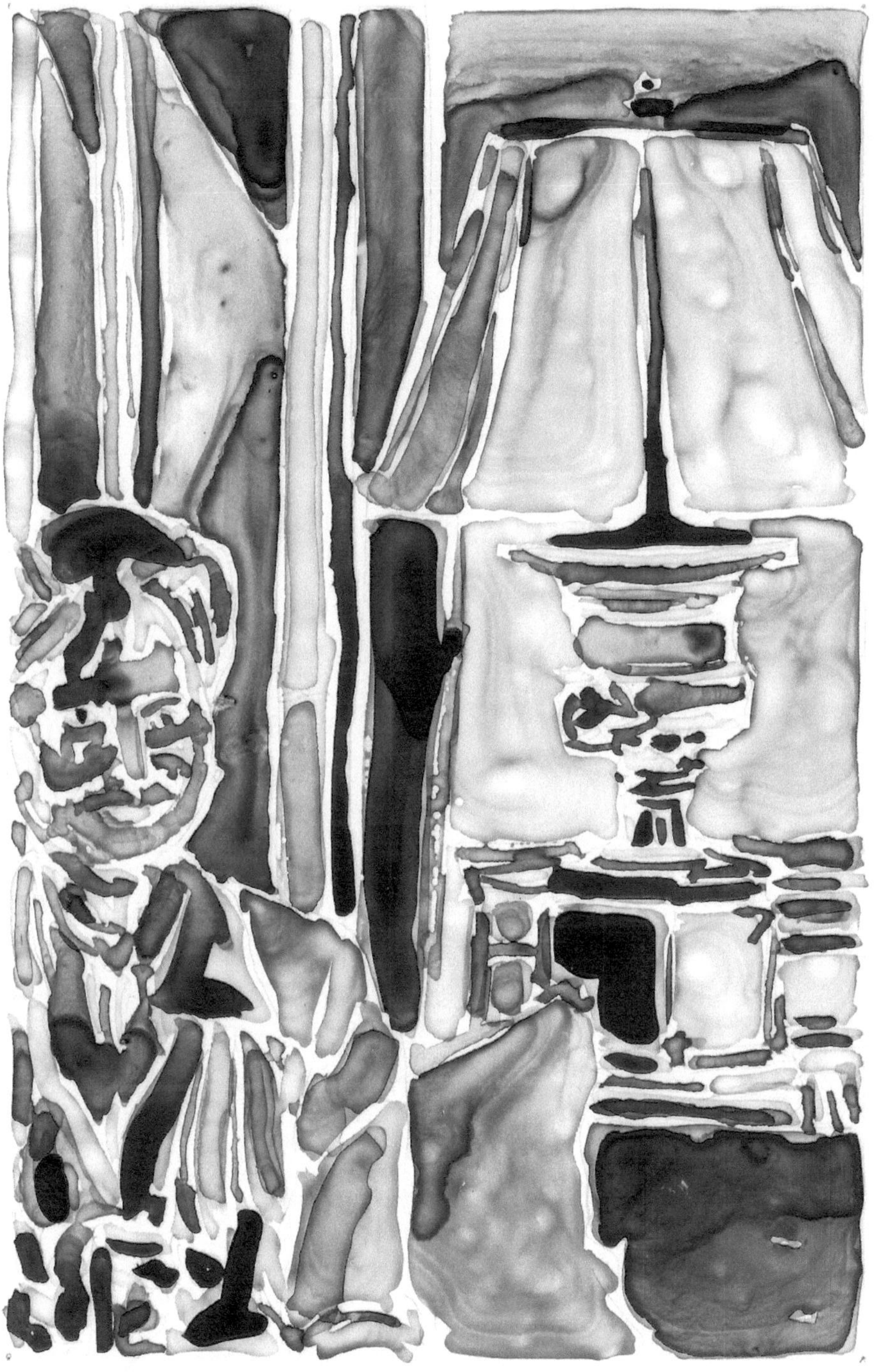

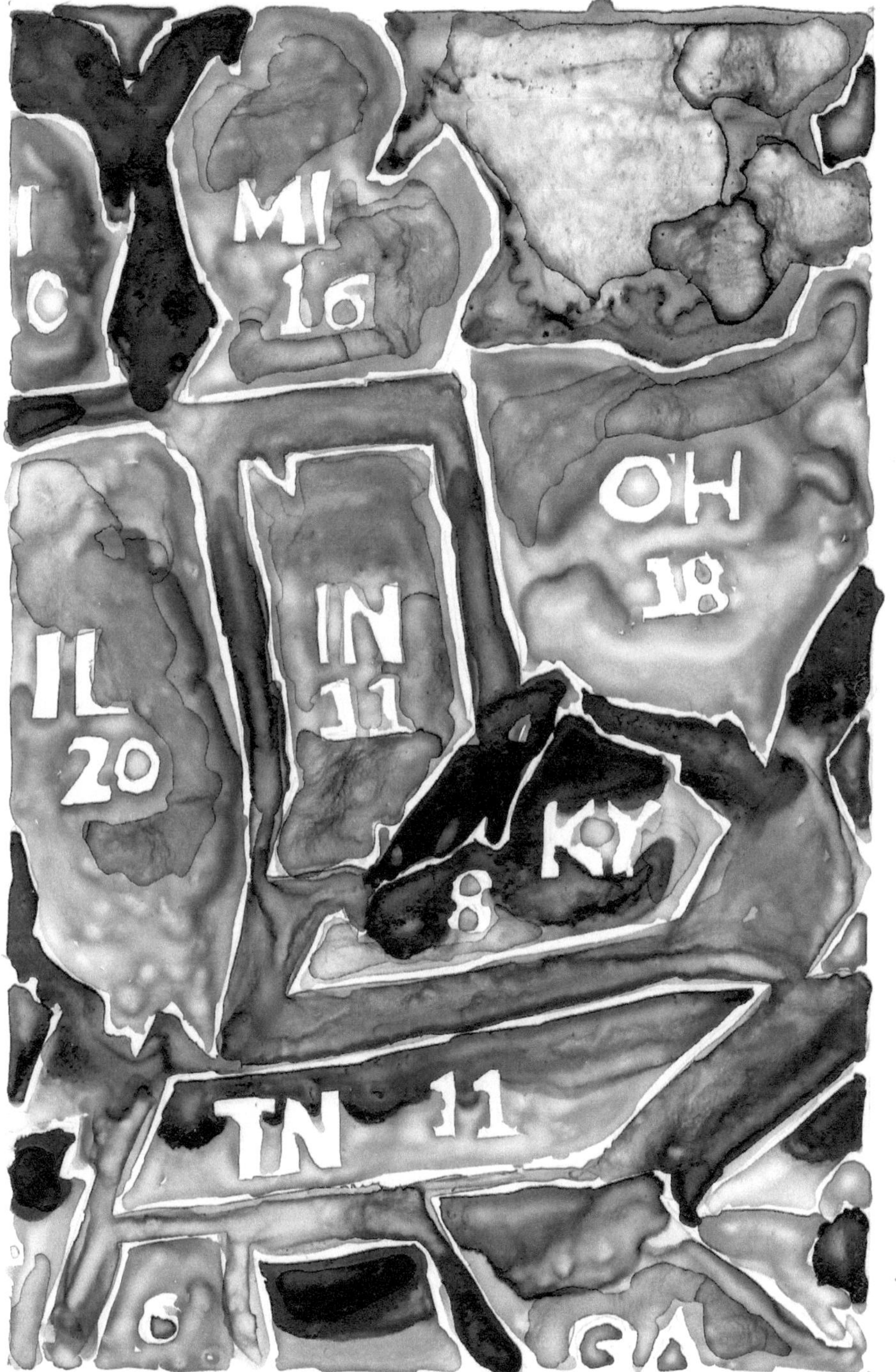
MI
16
OH
18
IN
11
IL
20
KY
8
TN 11

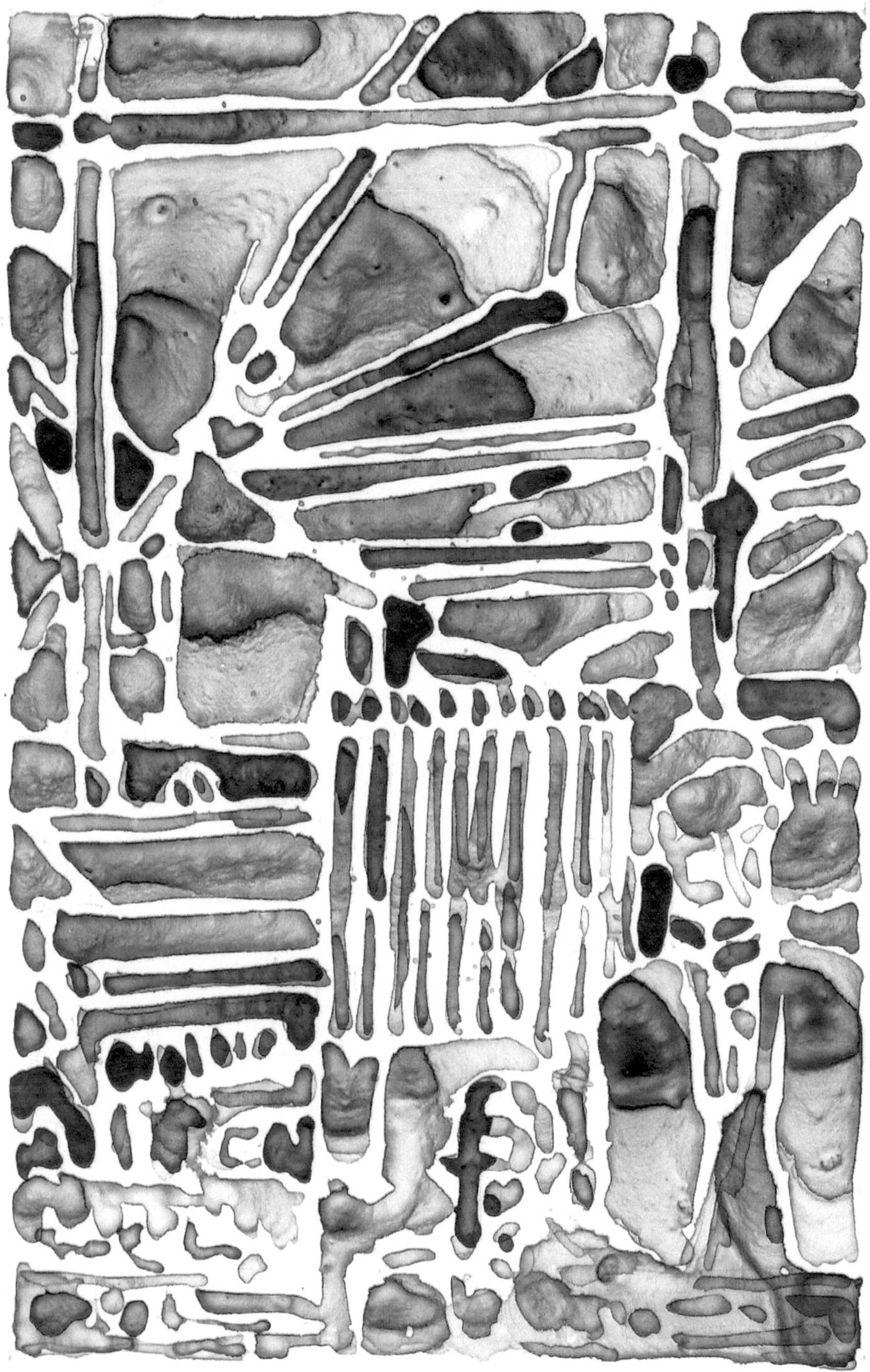

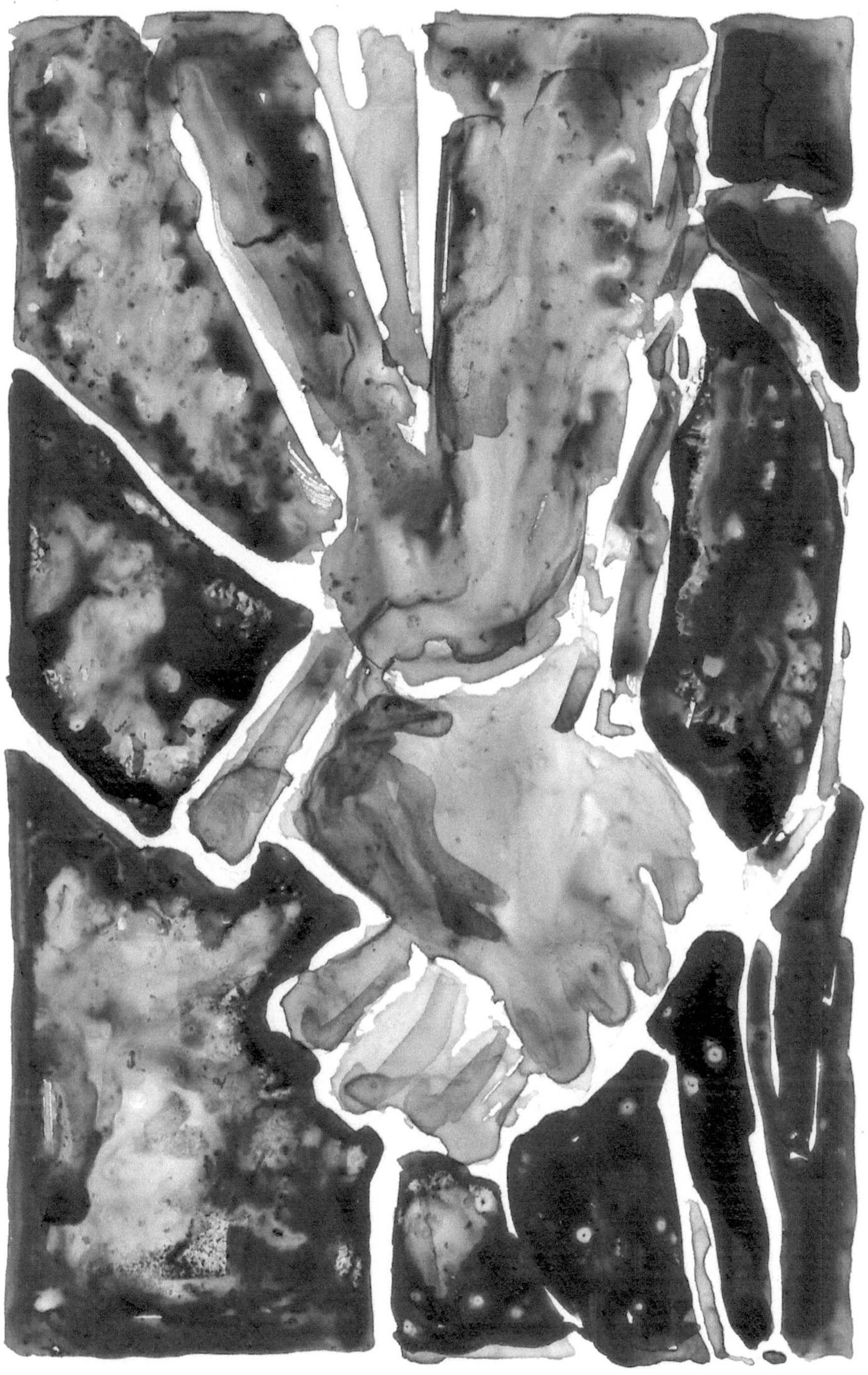

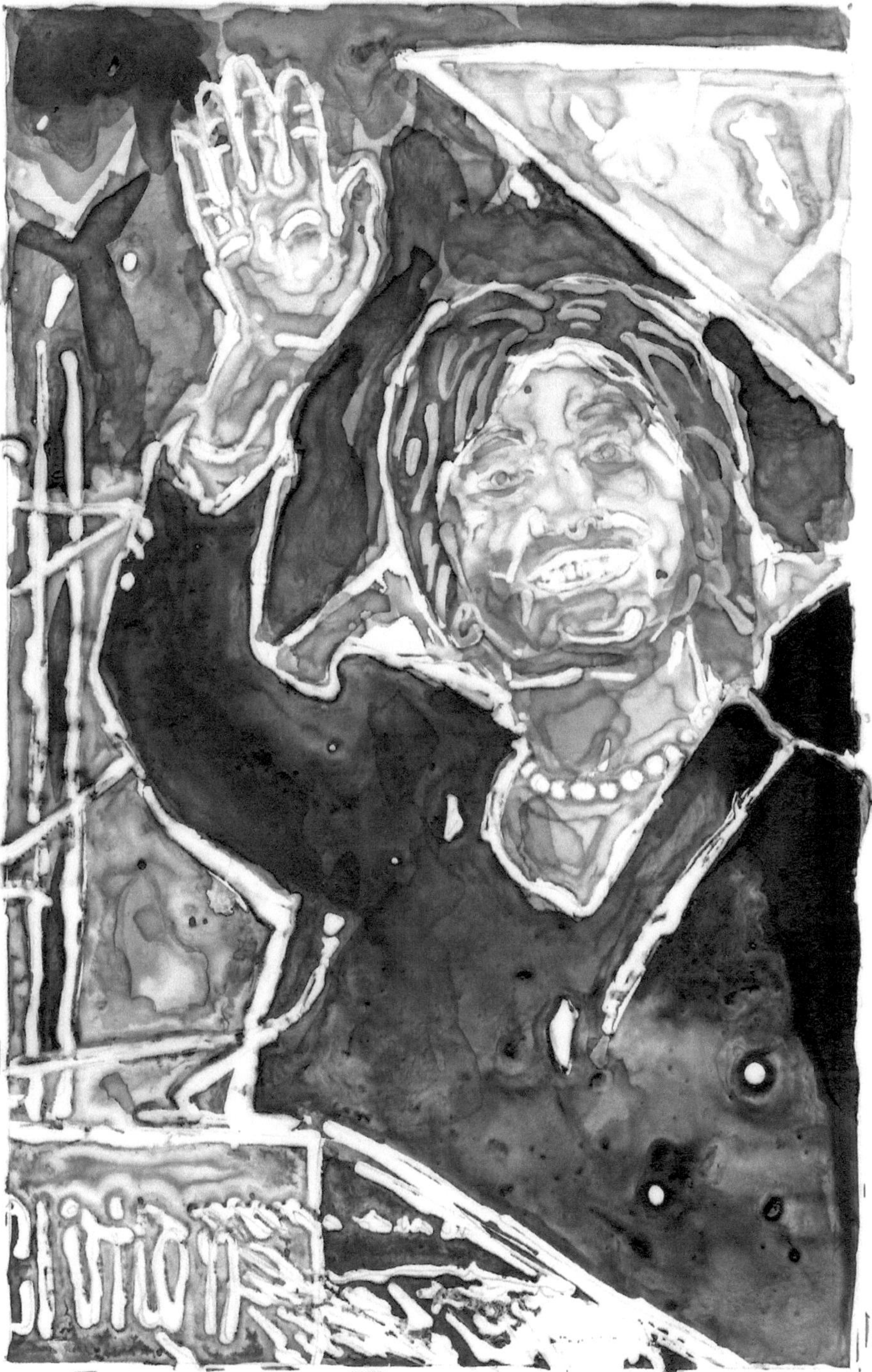

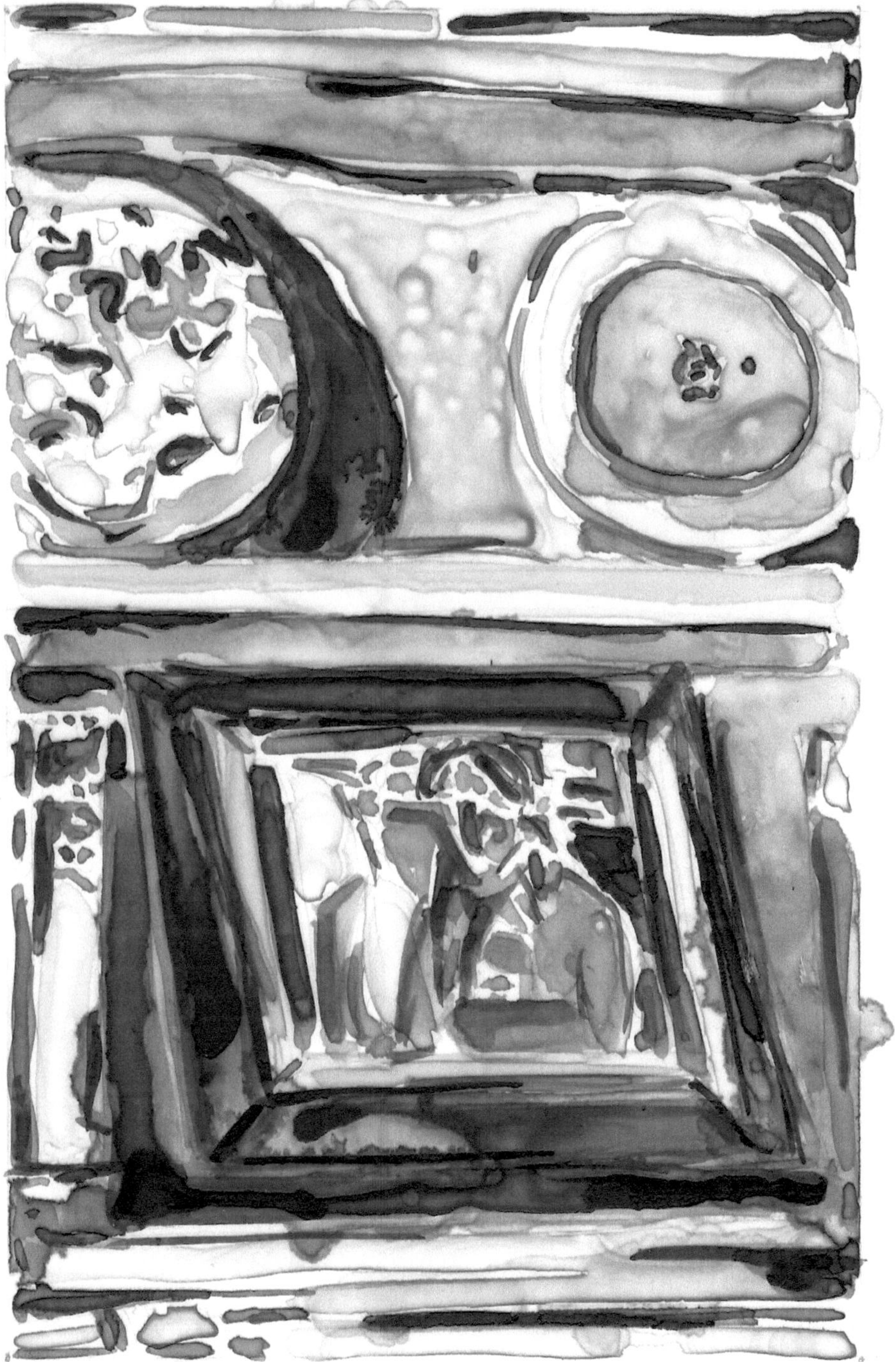

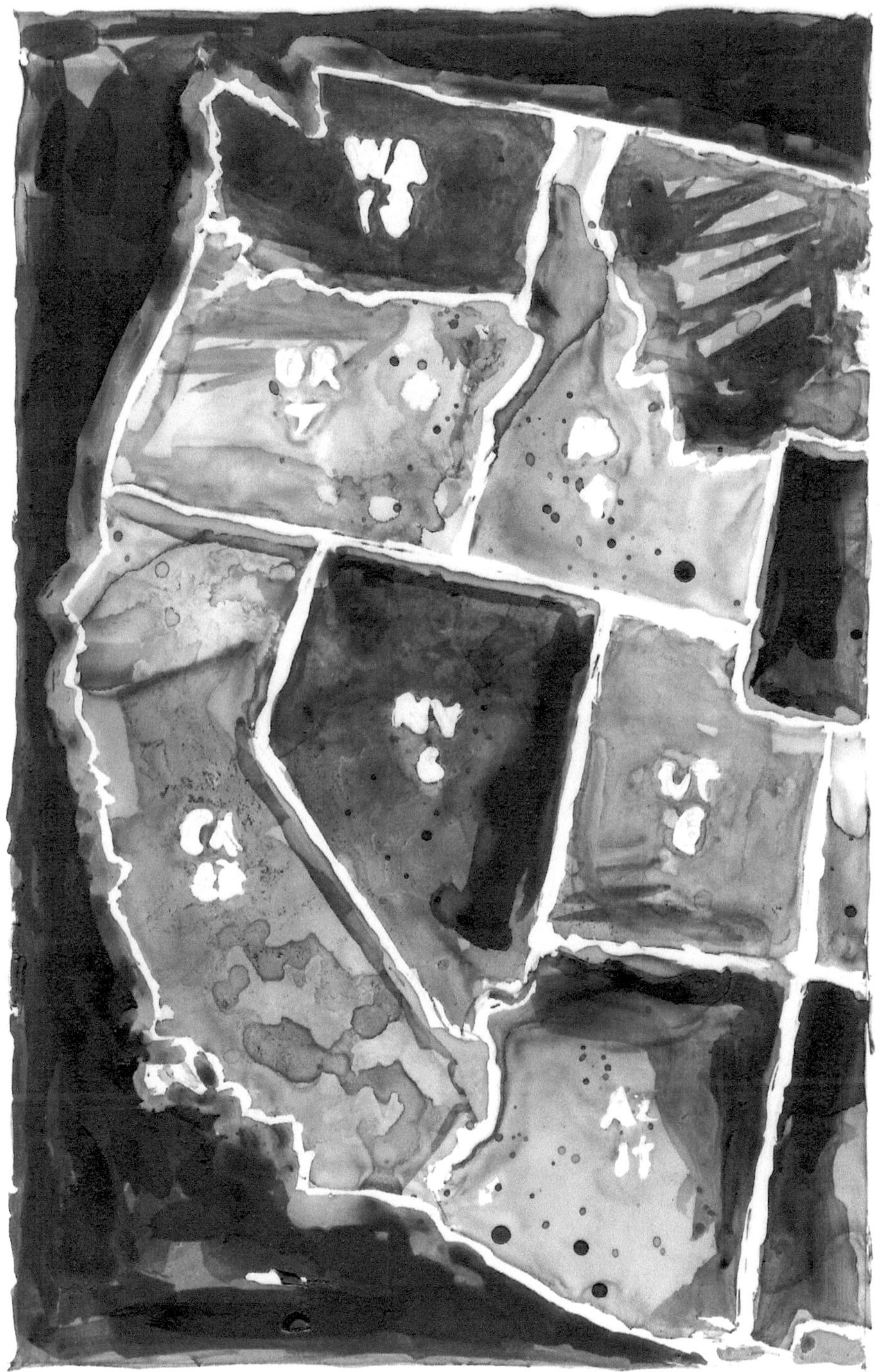
WA
OR
7
NV
6
CA
UT
AZ
11

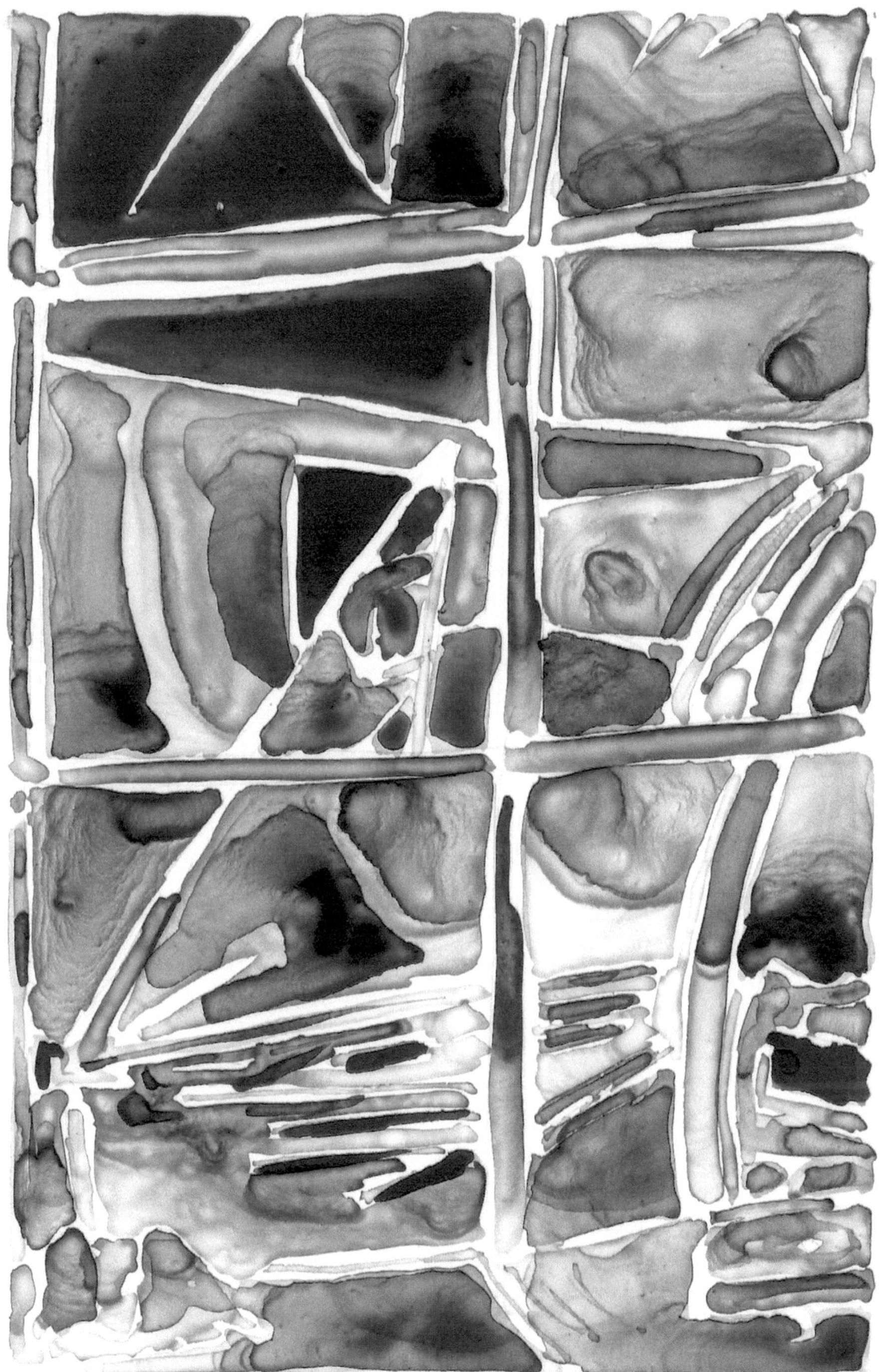

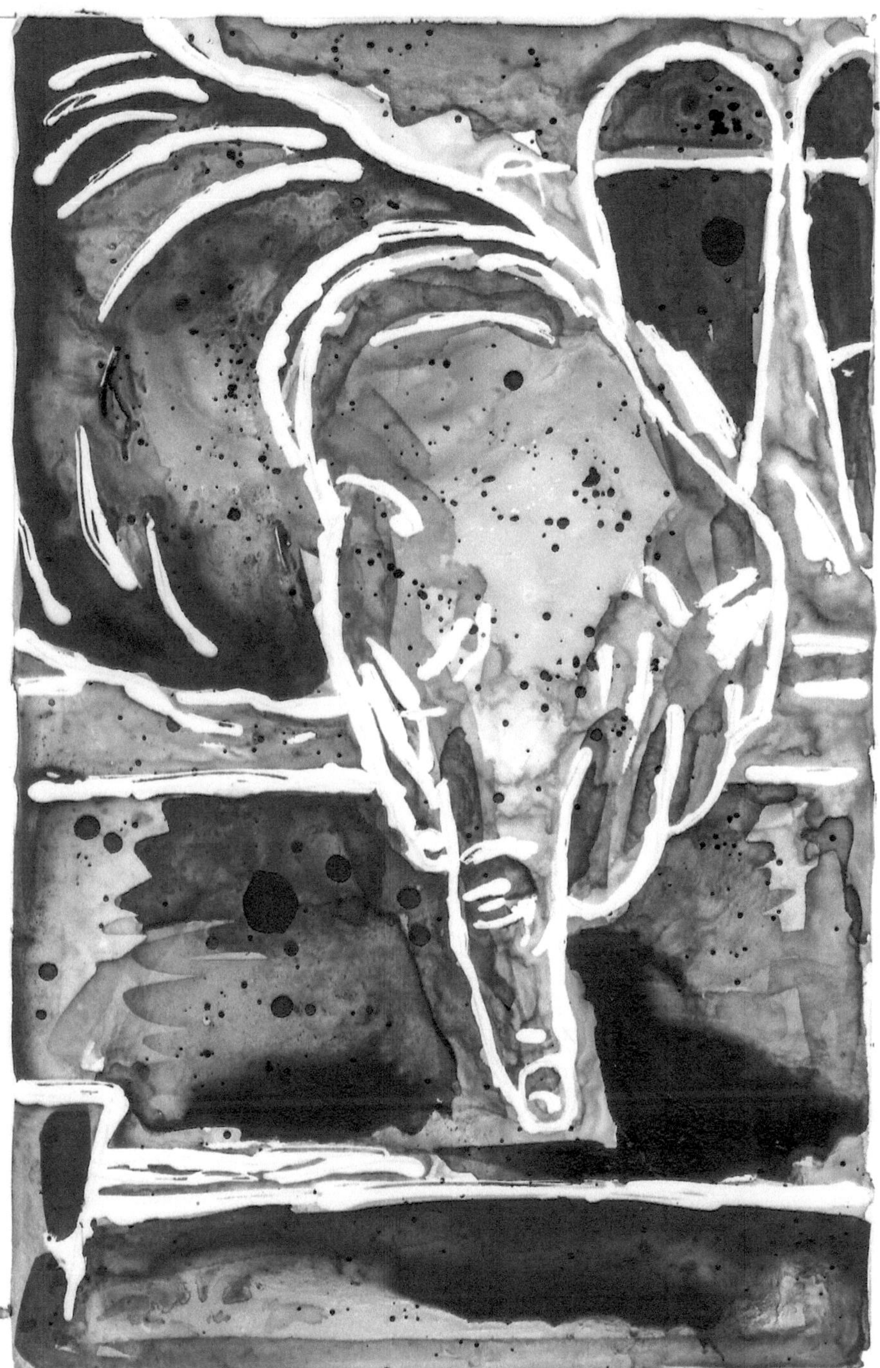

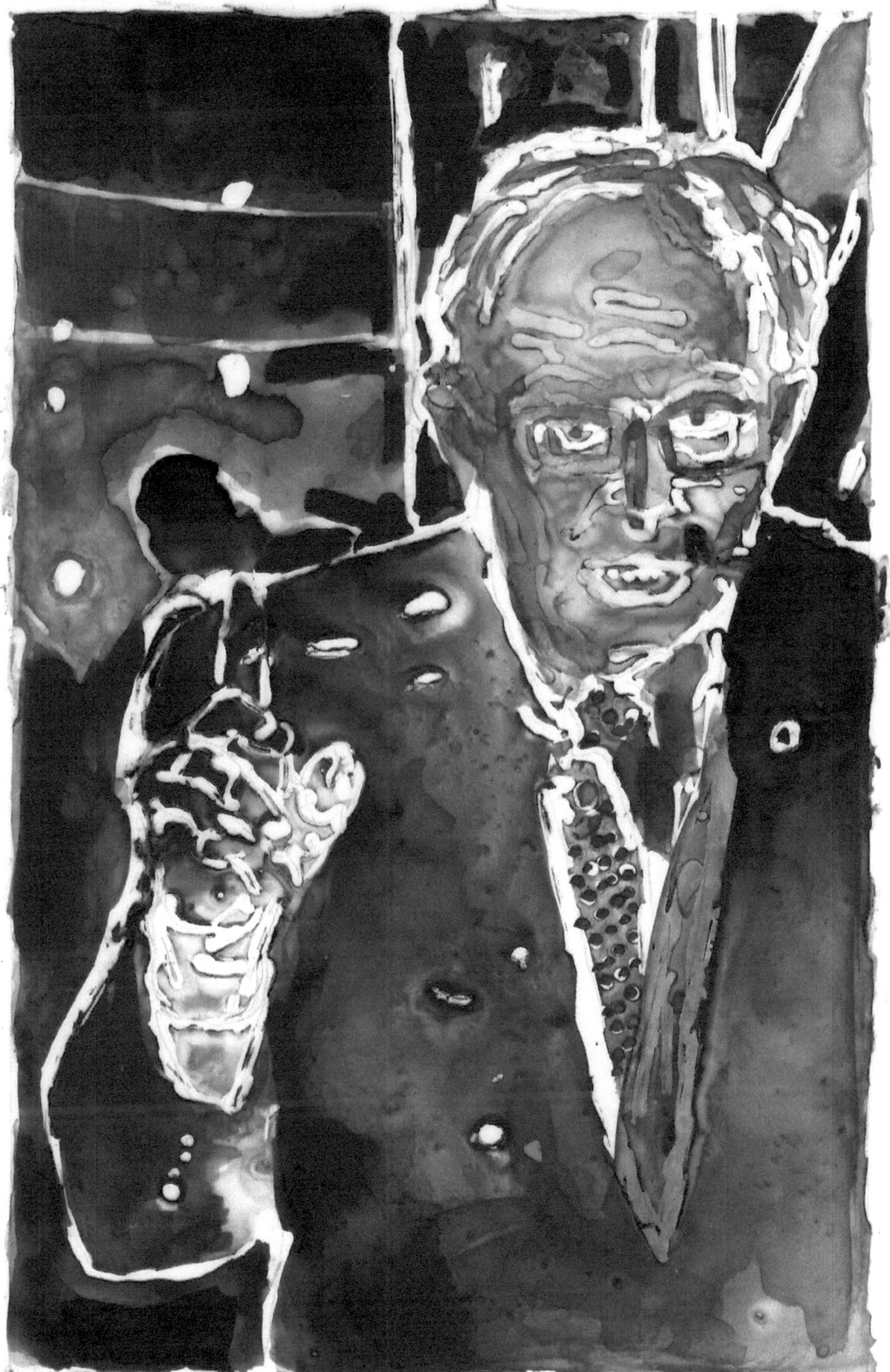

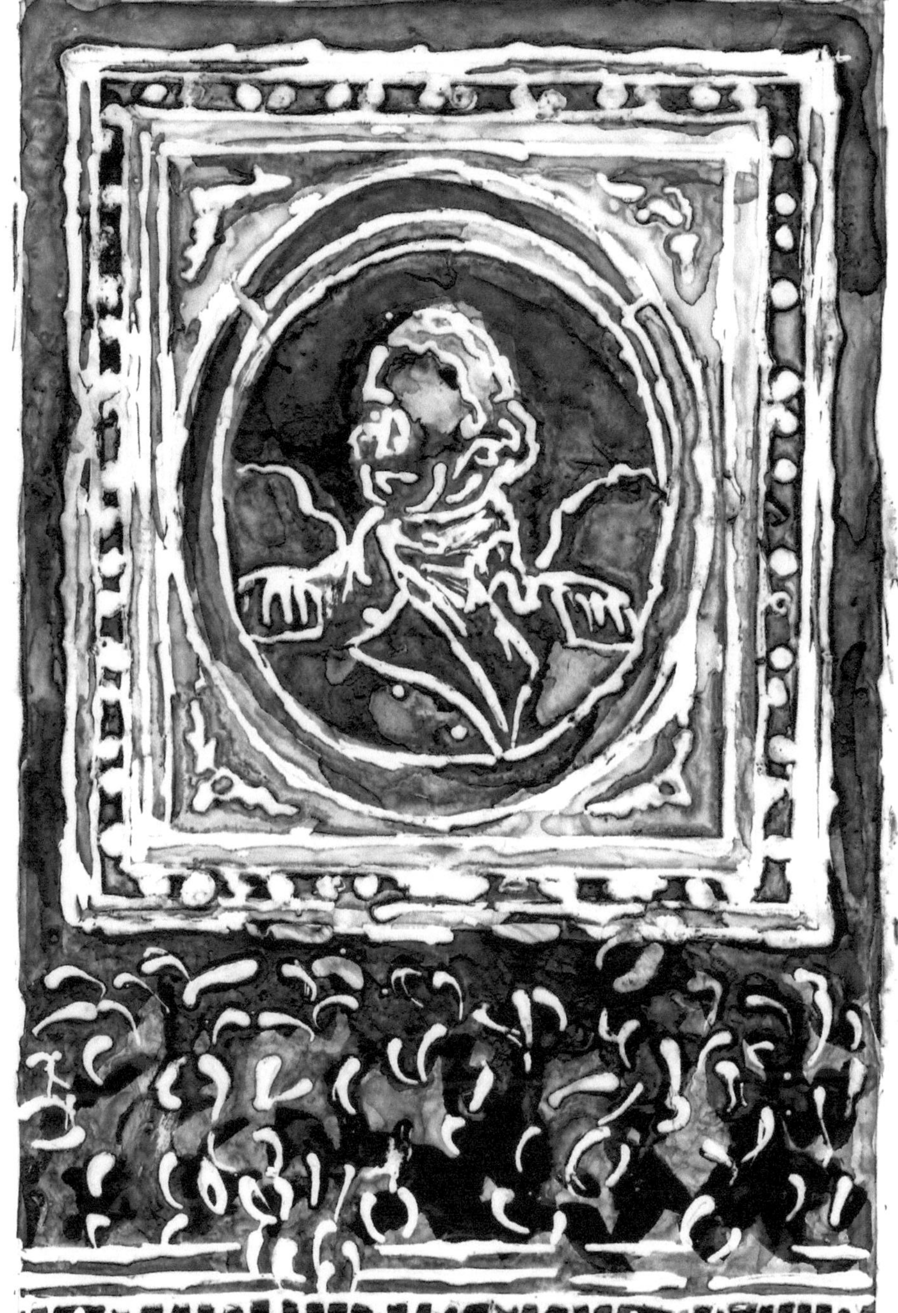

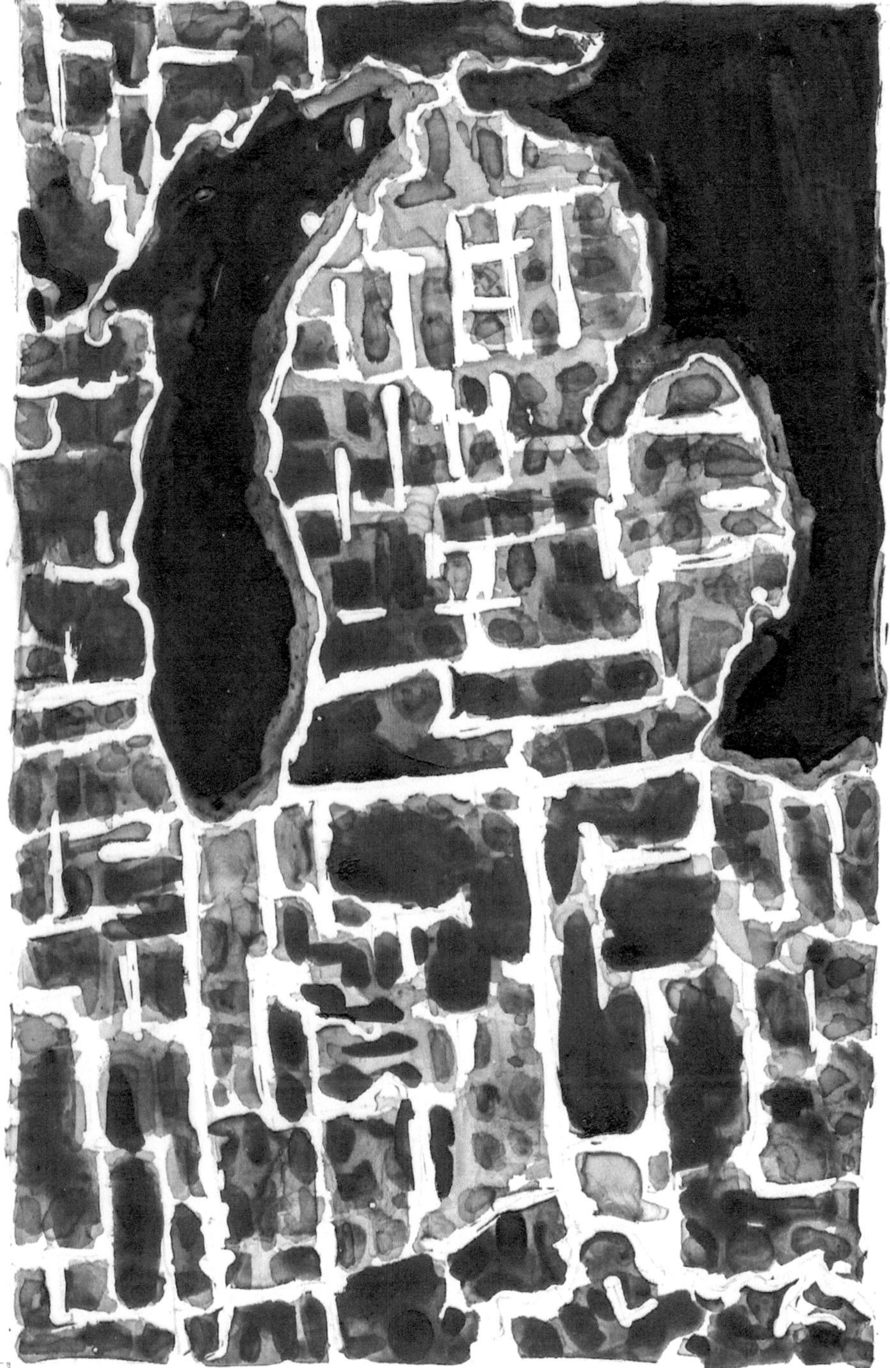

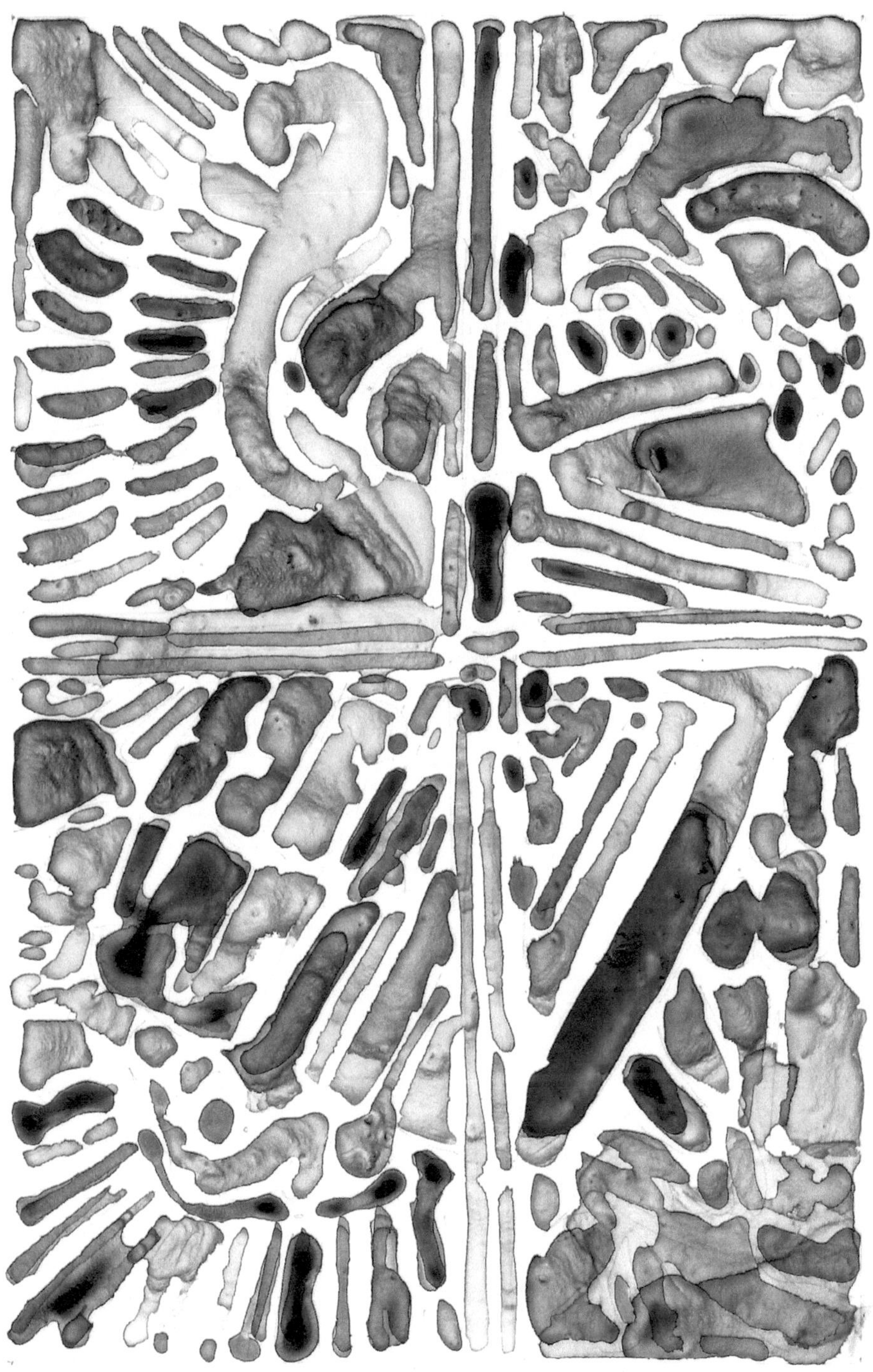

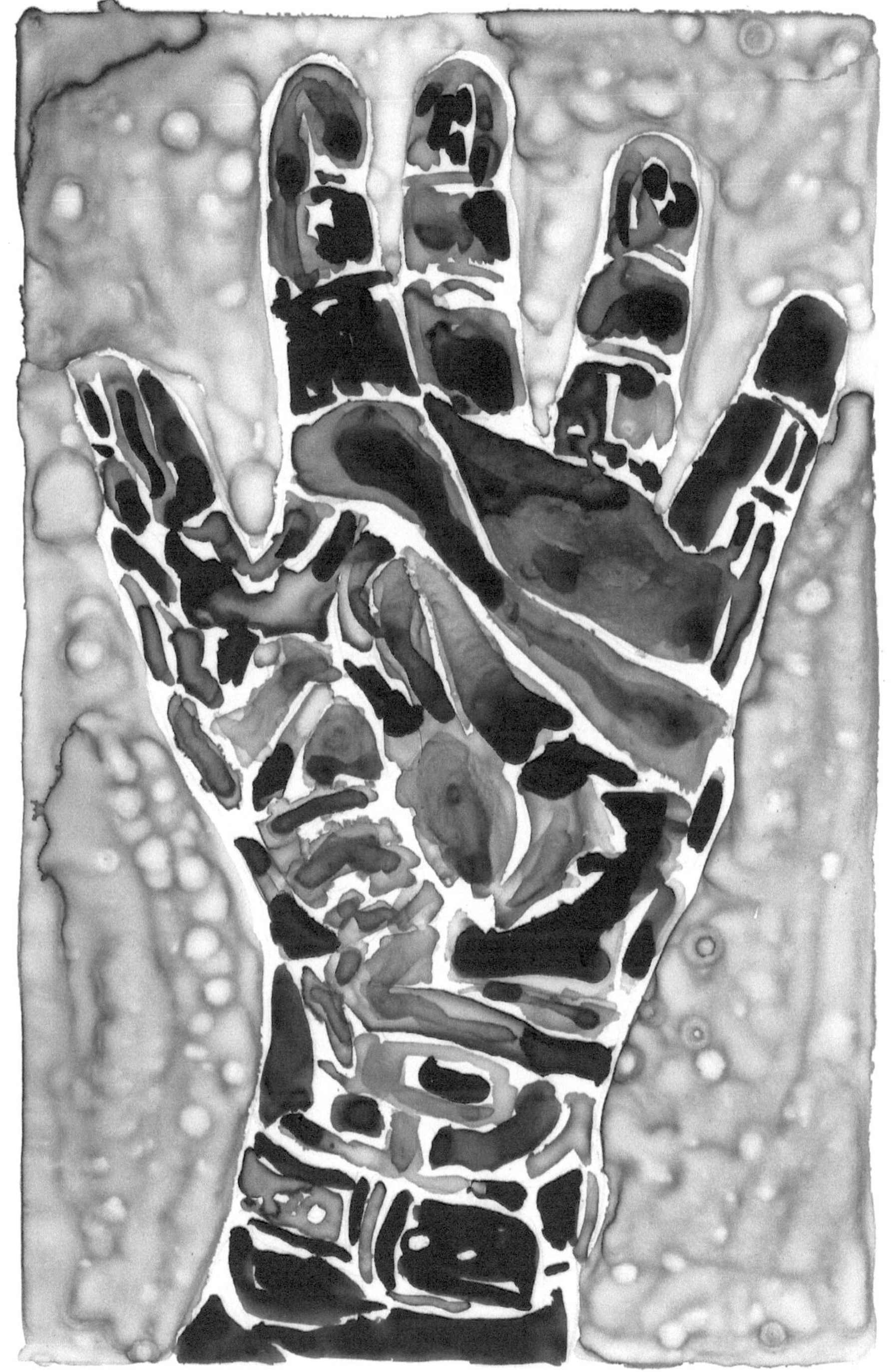

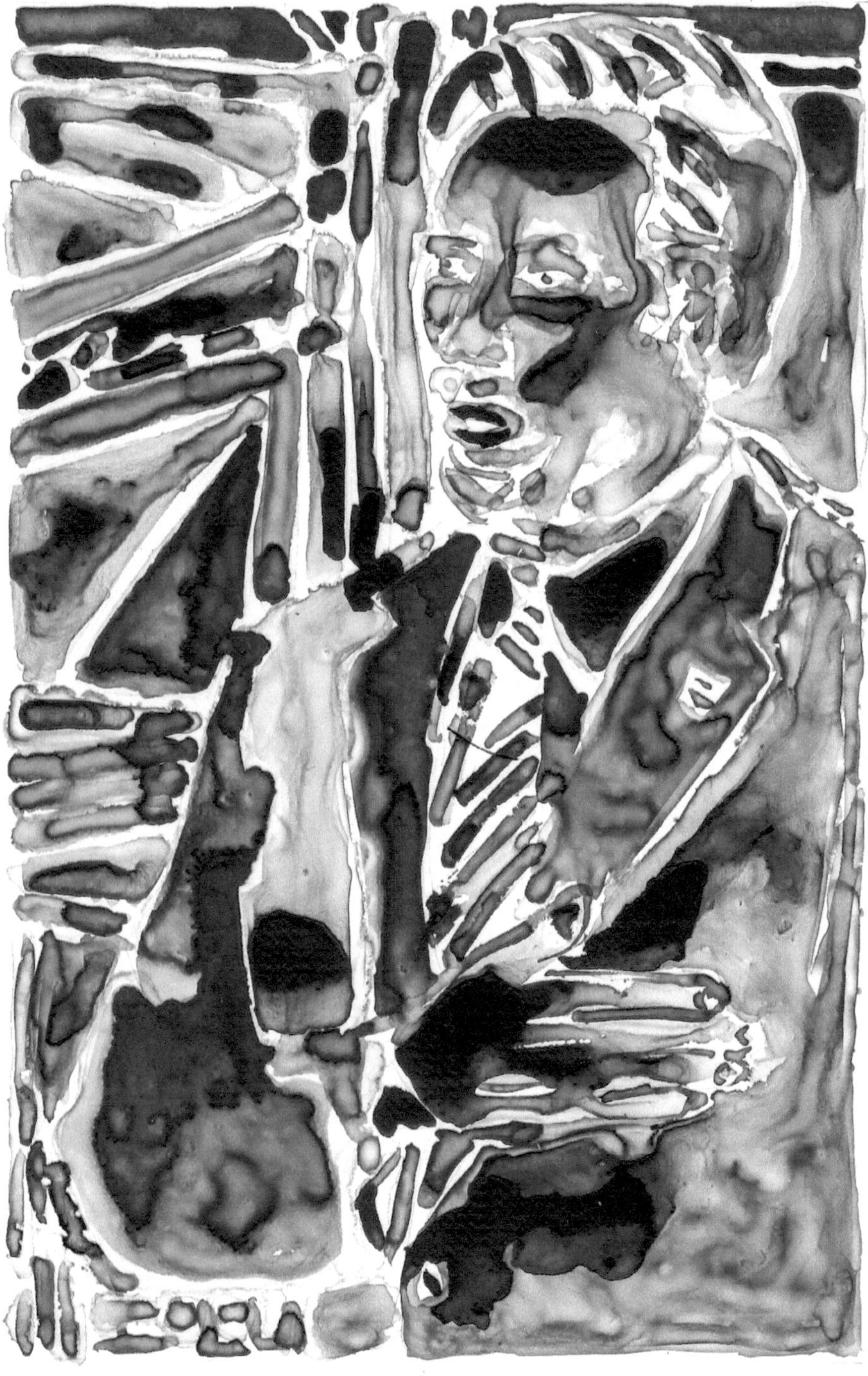

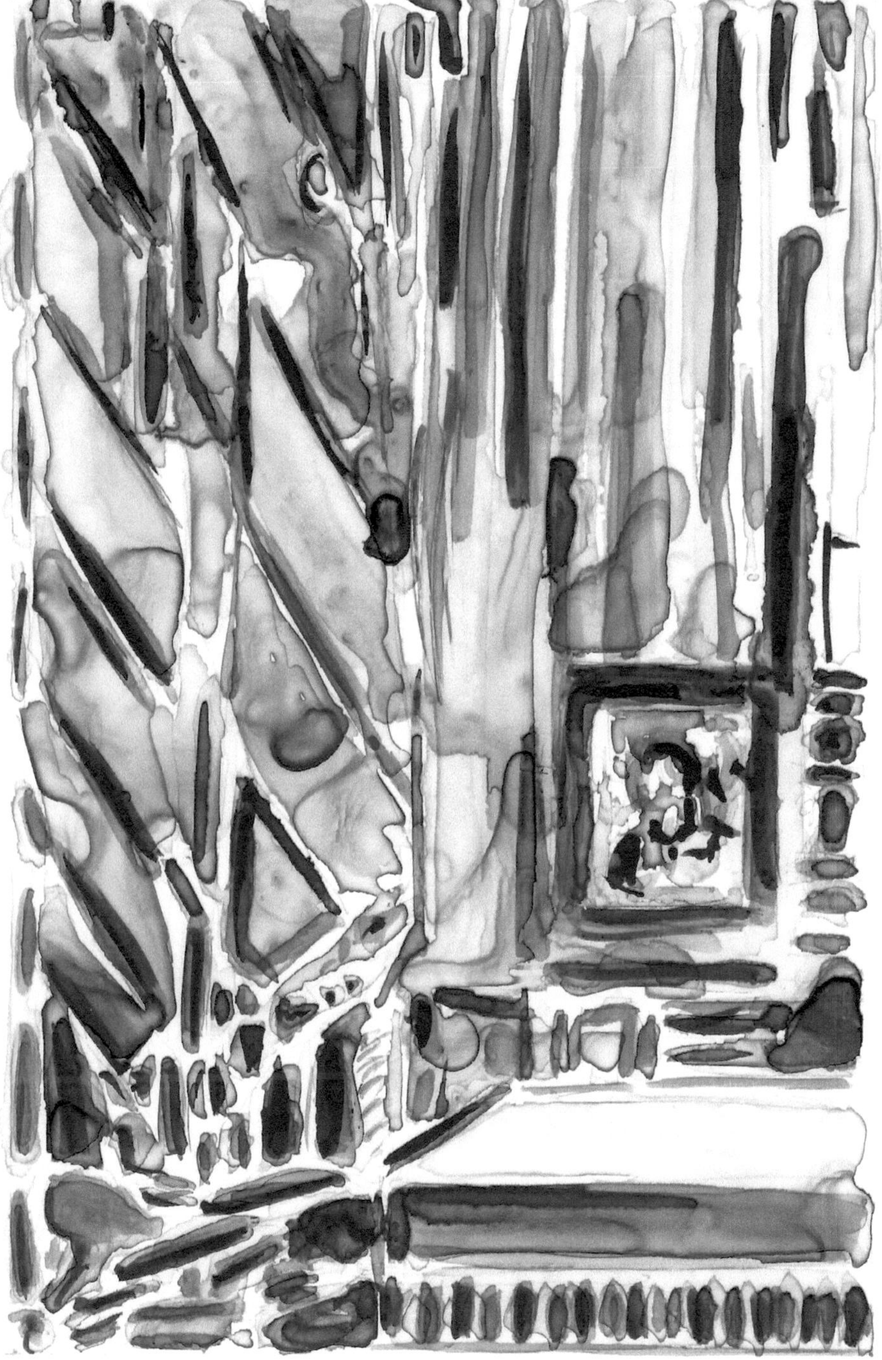

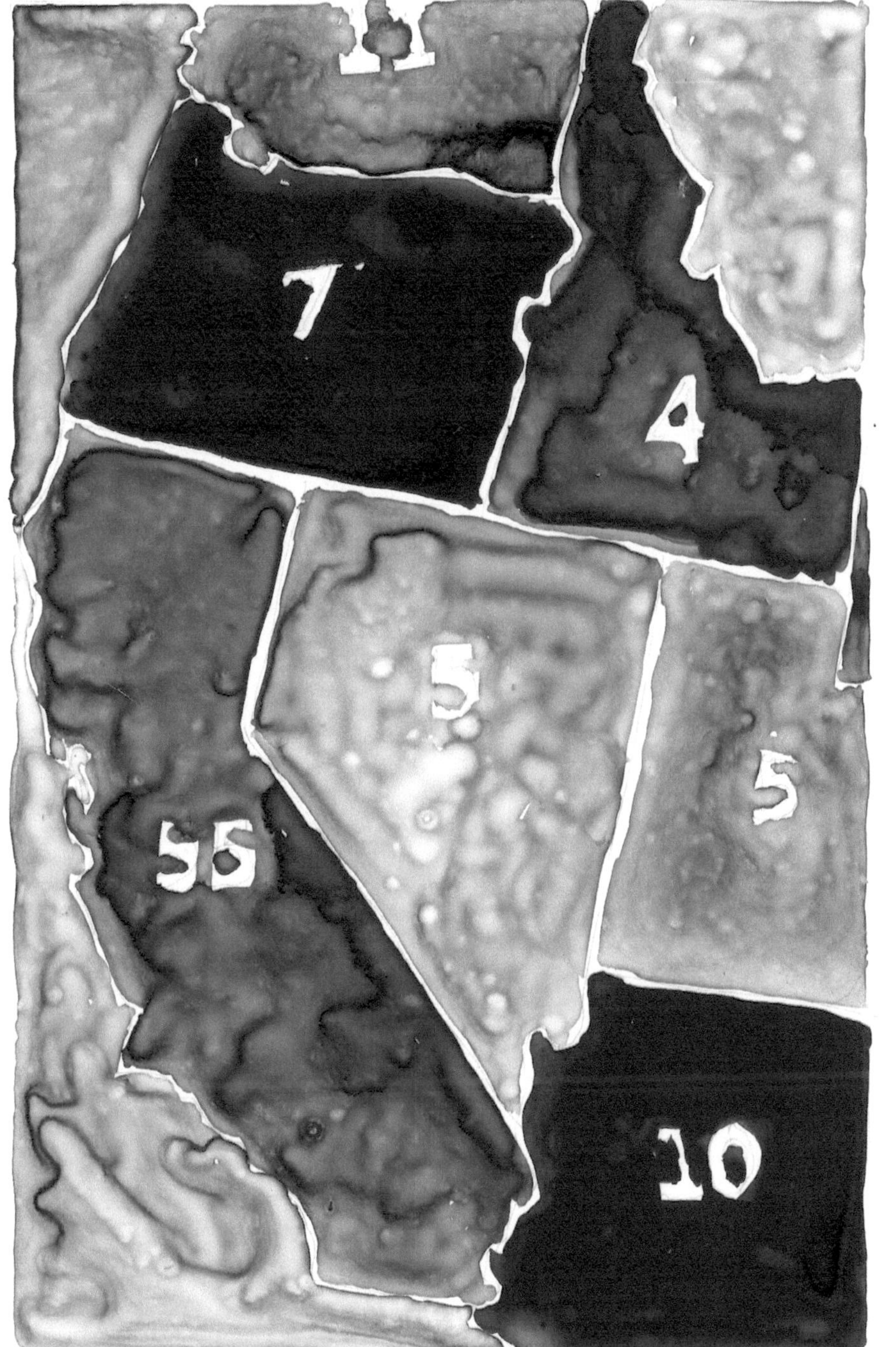
7
4
5
5
55
10

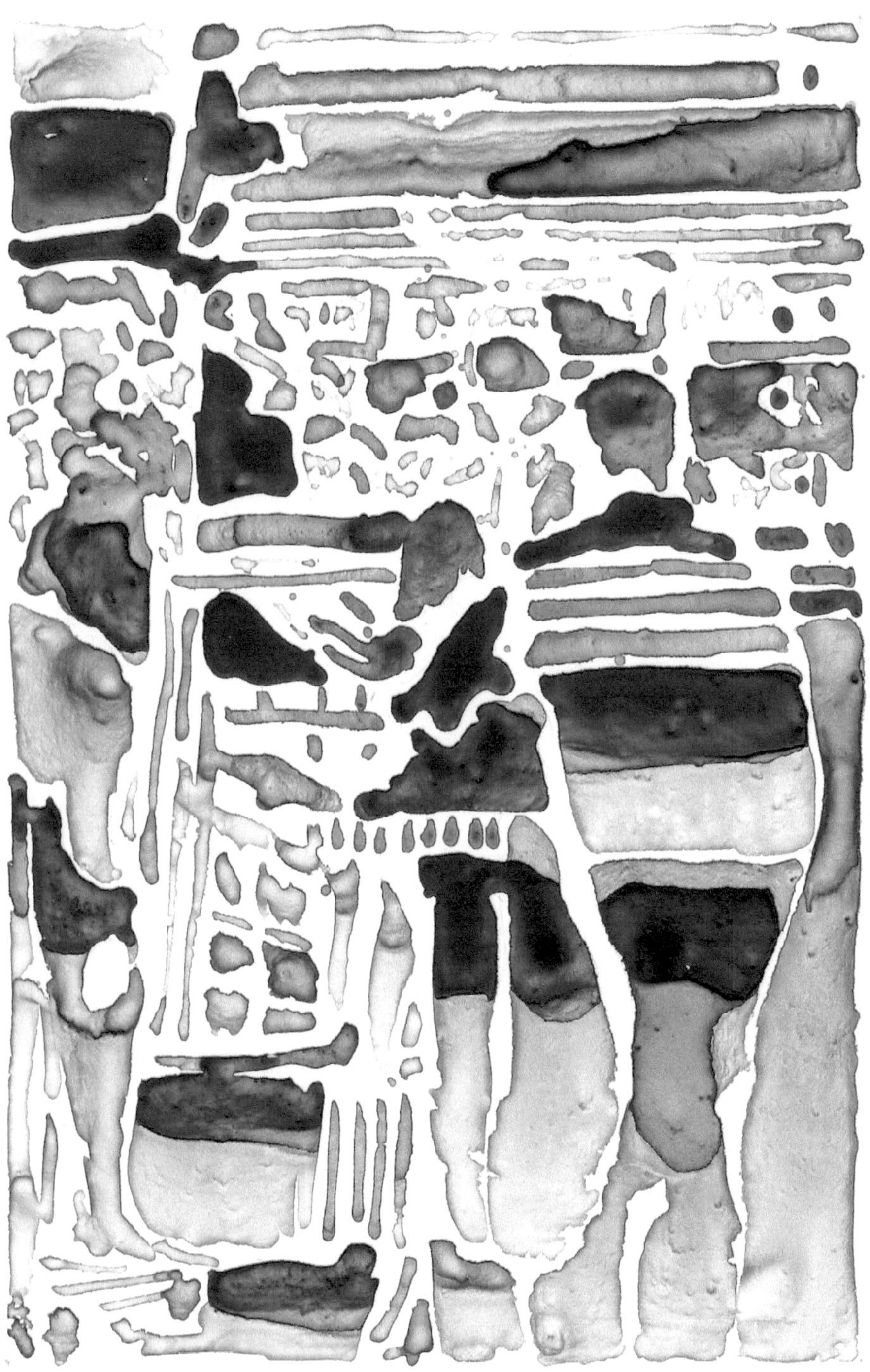

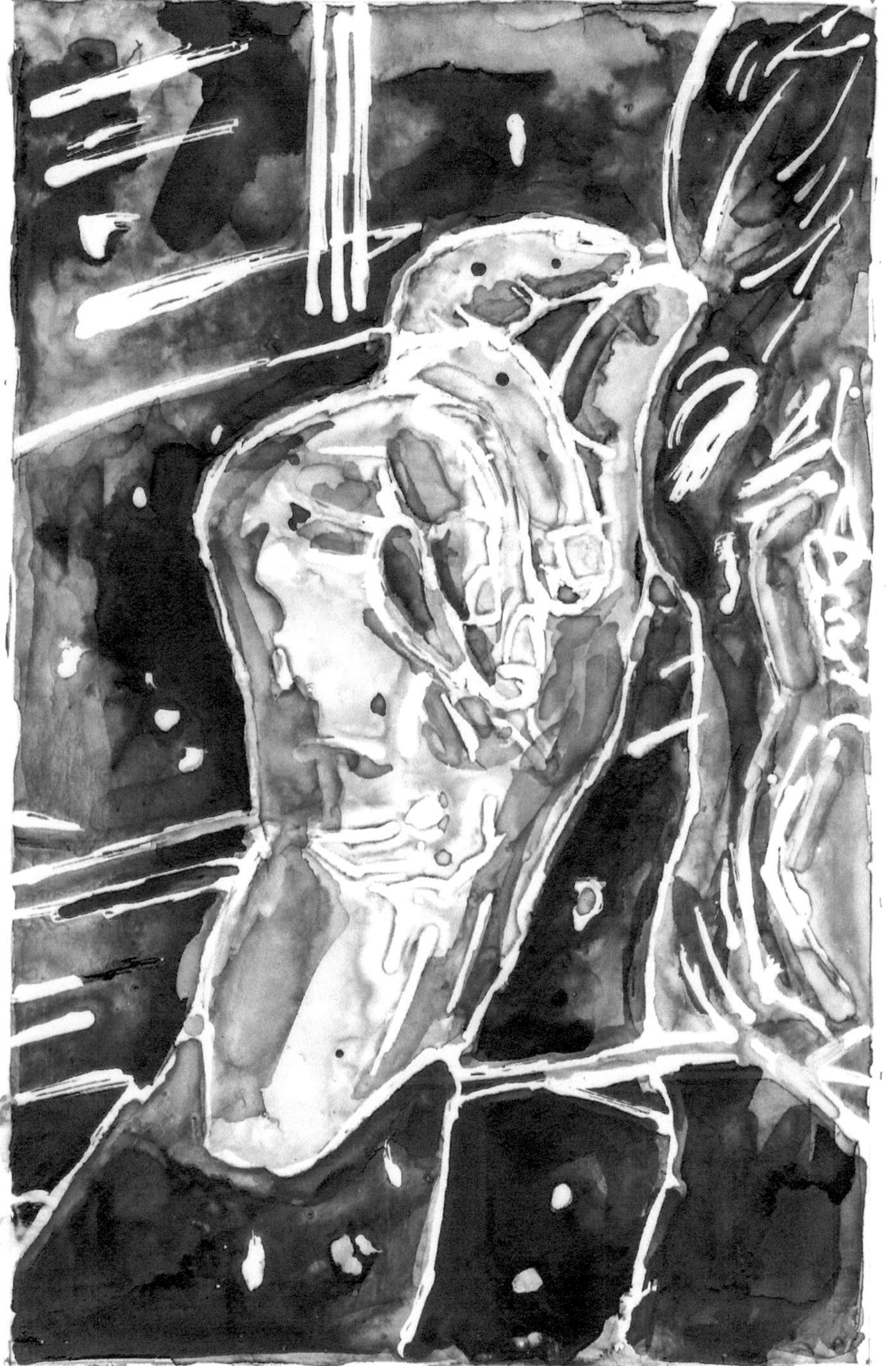

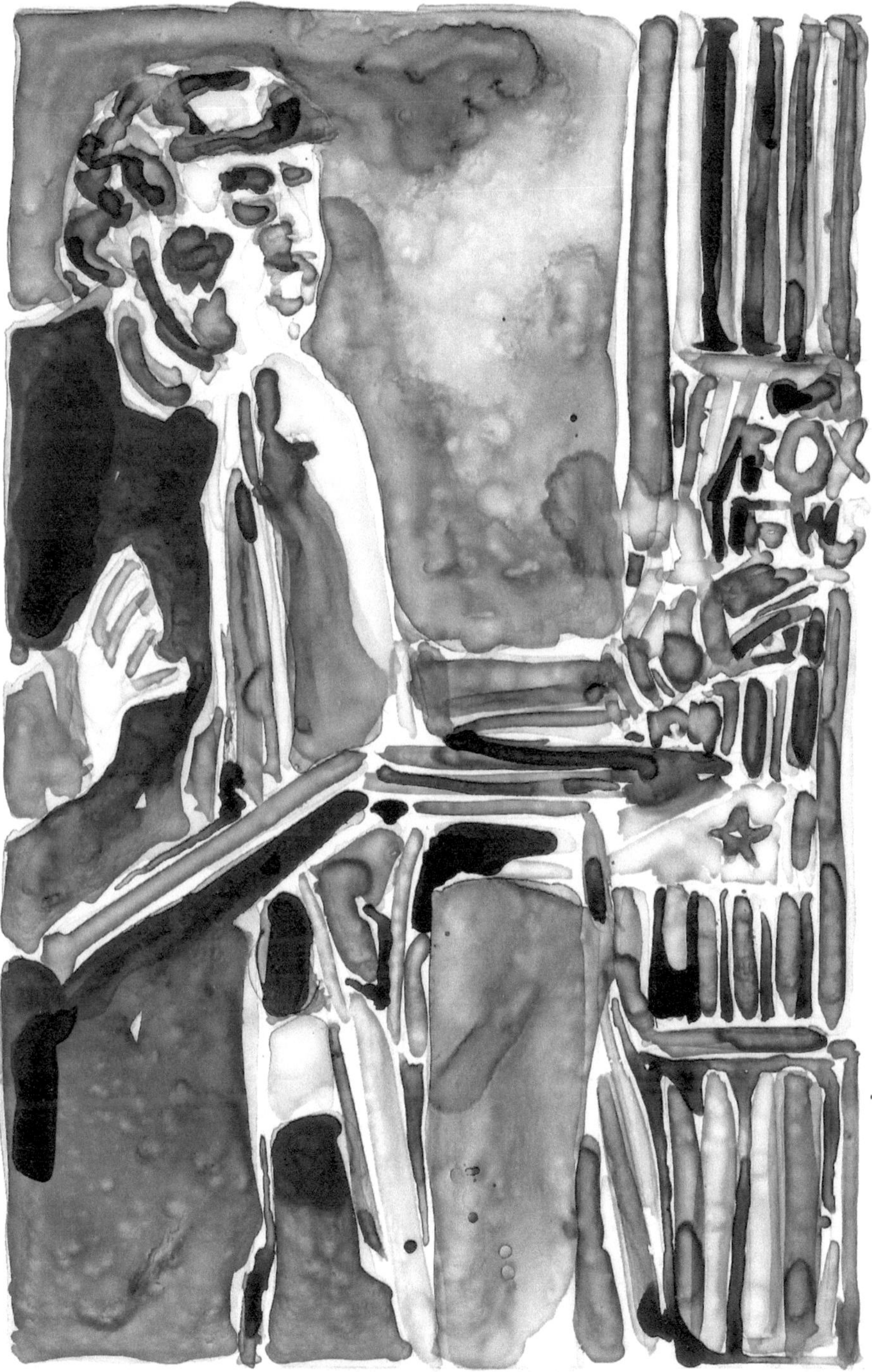

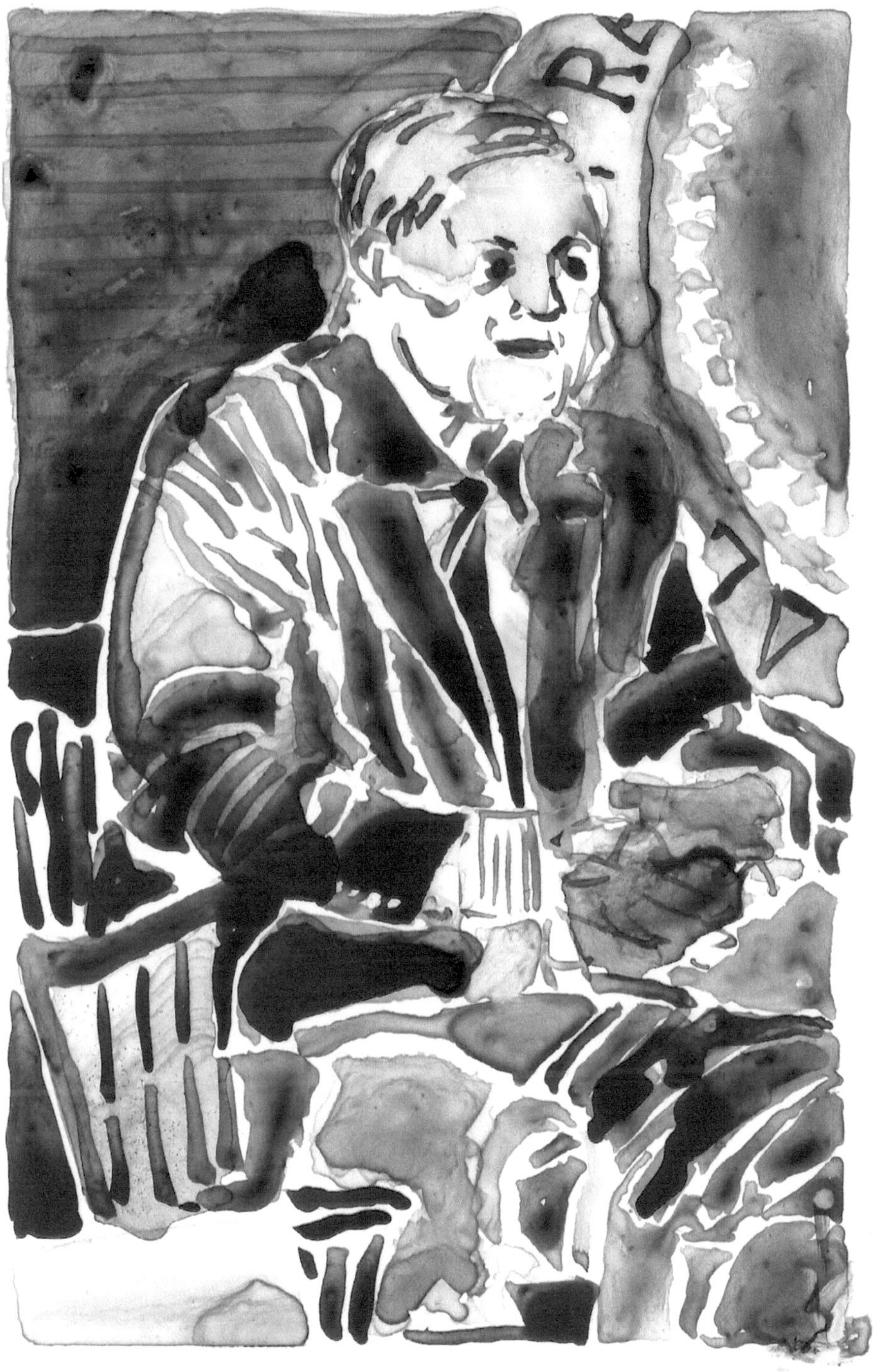

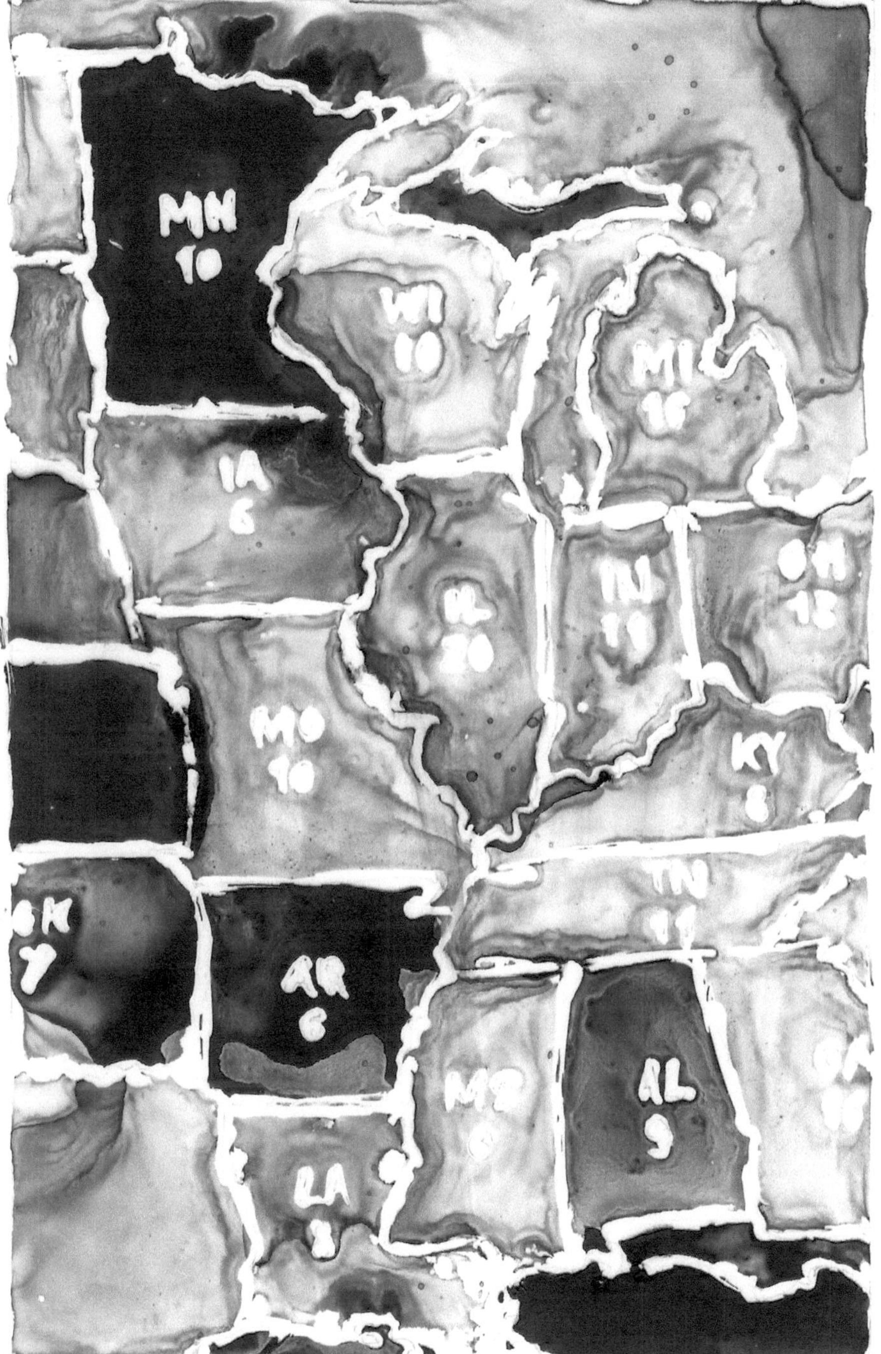
MN
10
WI
10
MI
16
IA
6
IL
20
IN
11
OH
18
MO
10
KY
8
TN
11
AR
6
AL
9
LA
8
MS

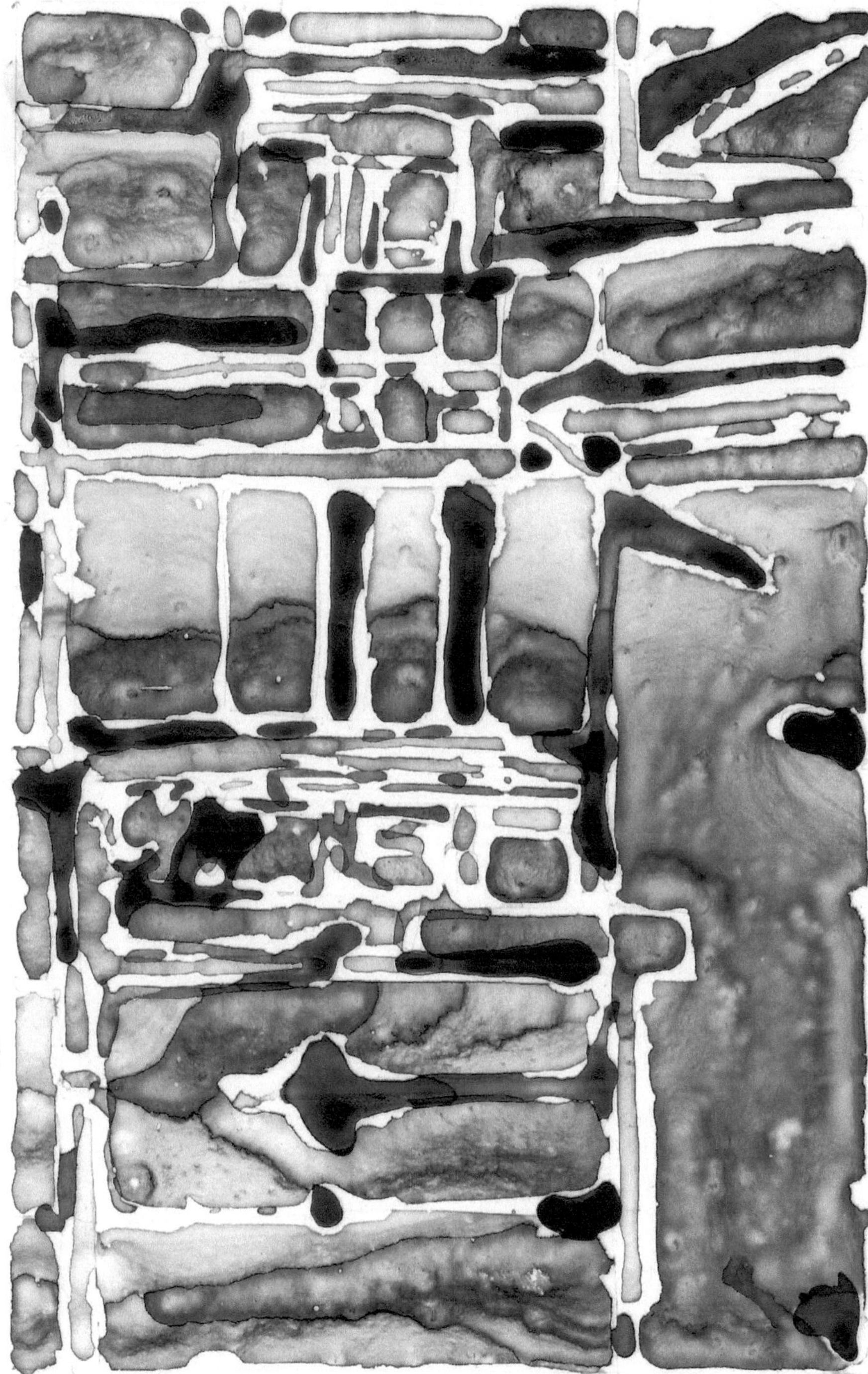

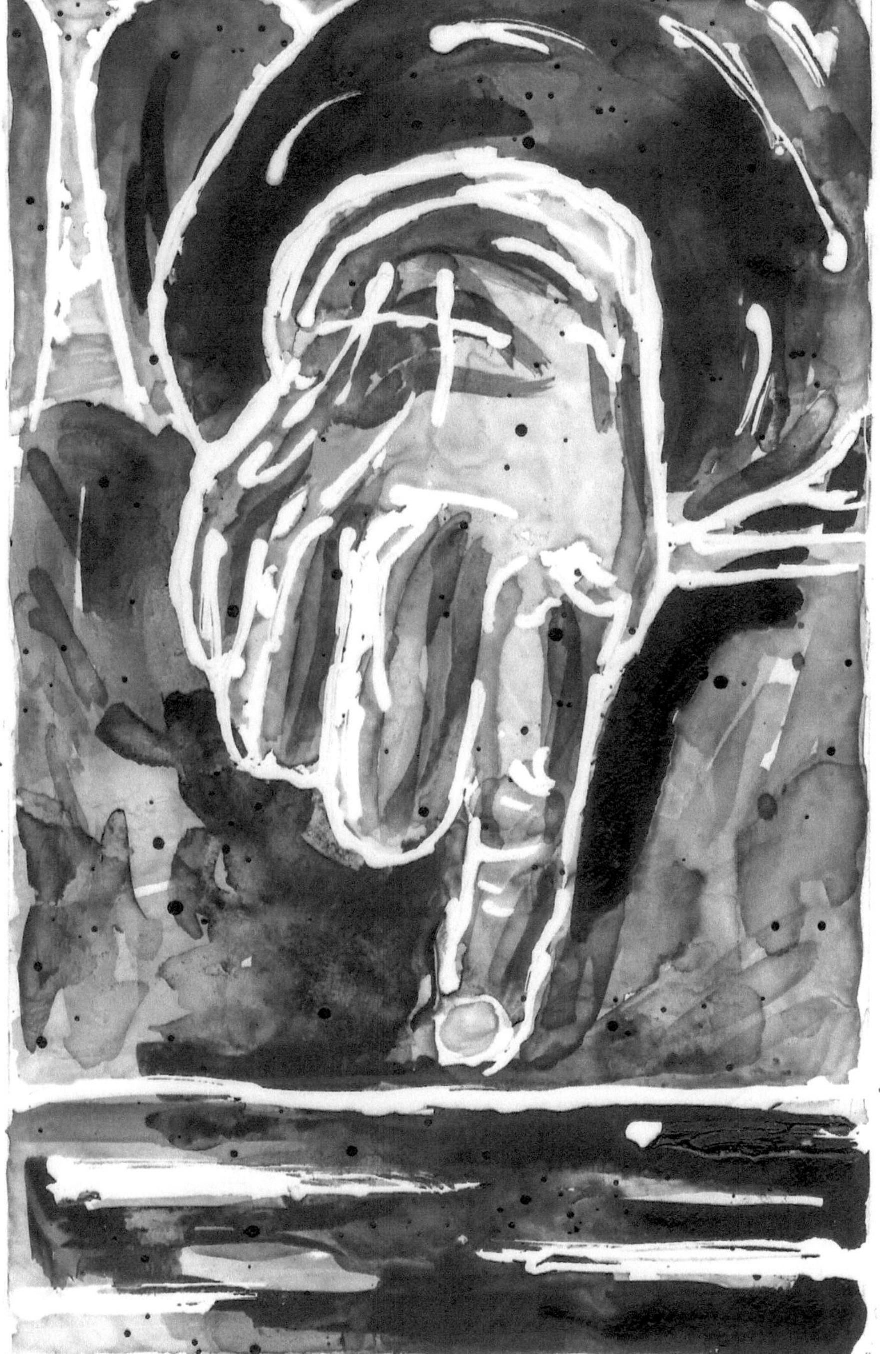

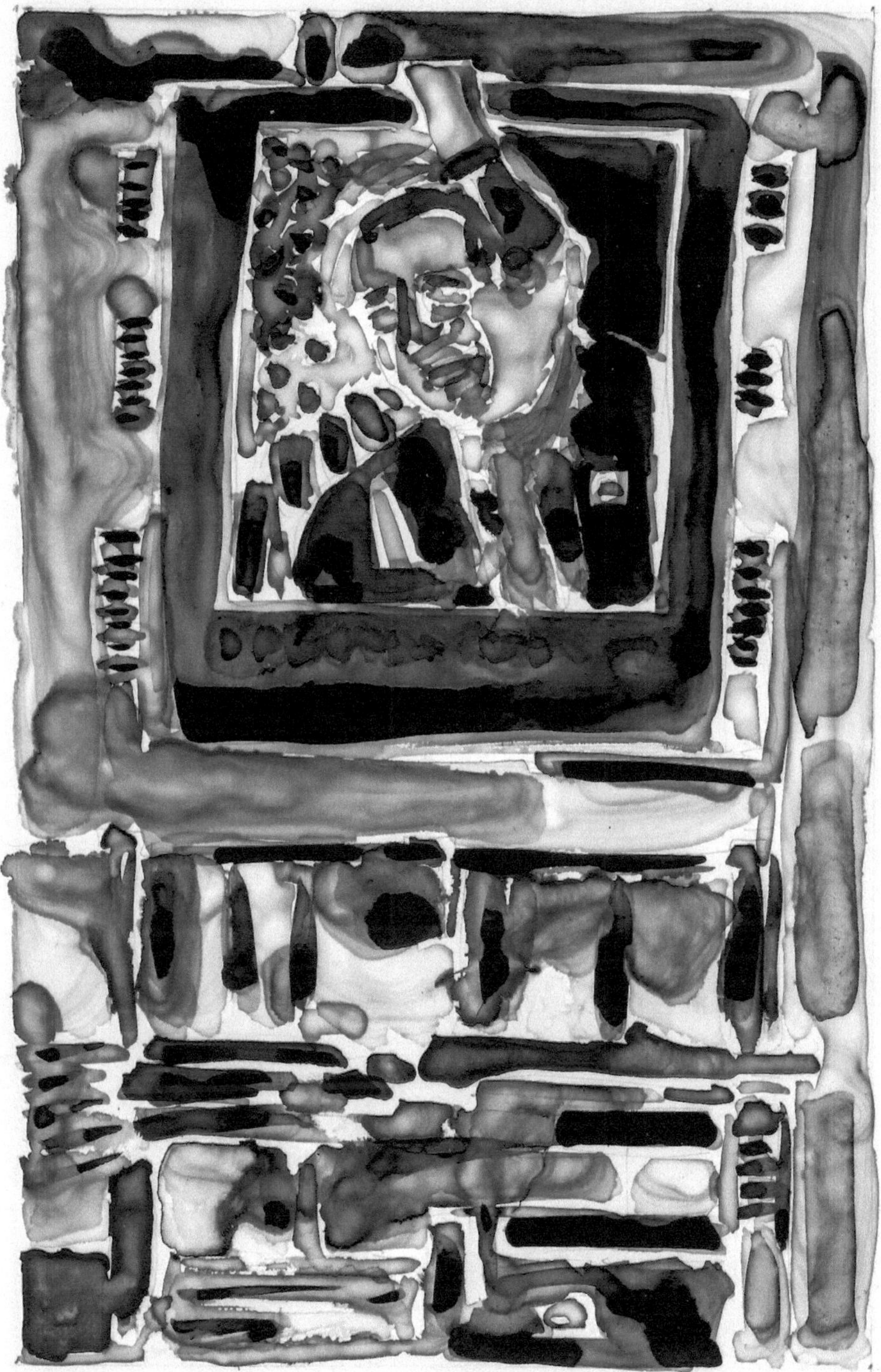

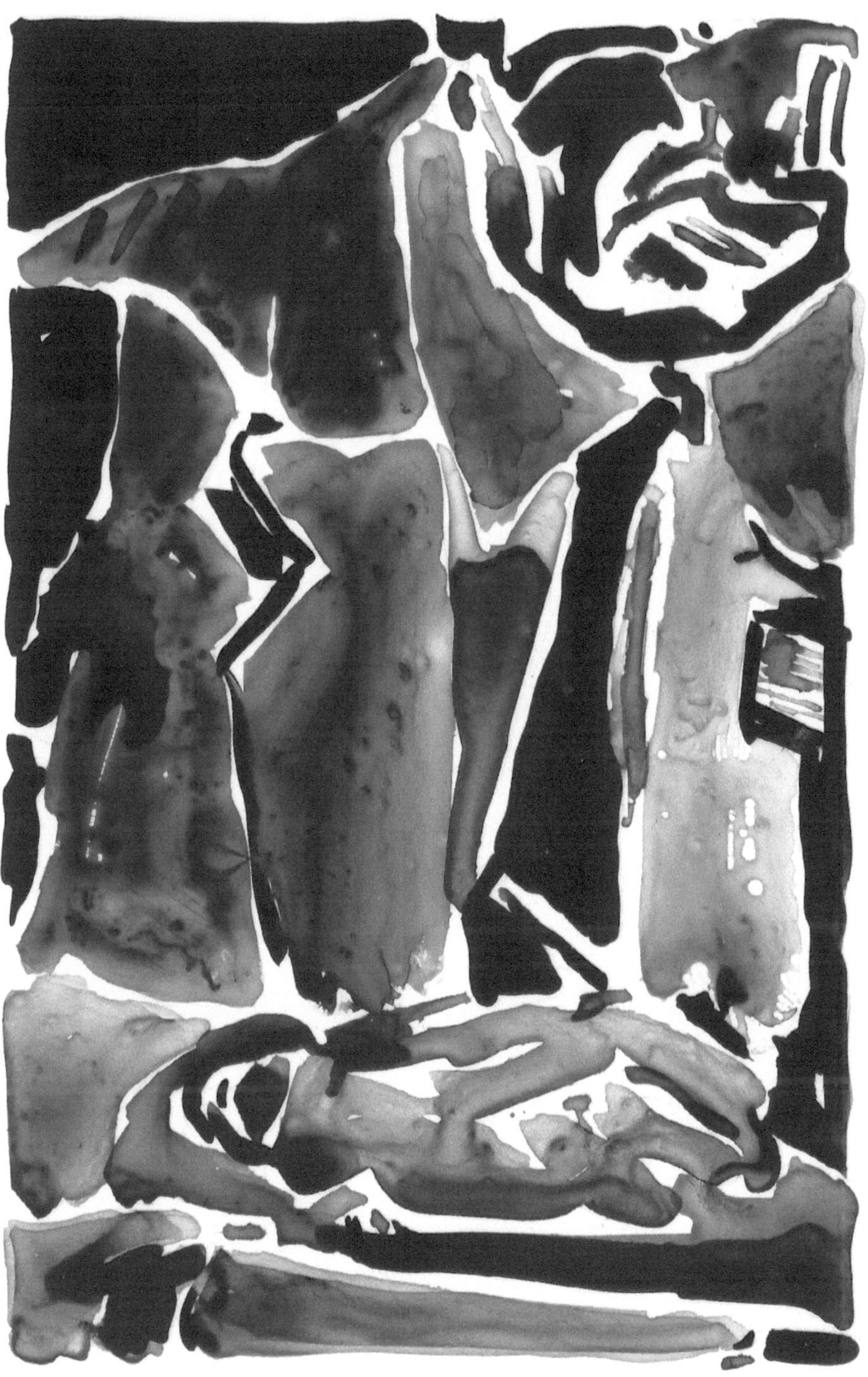

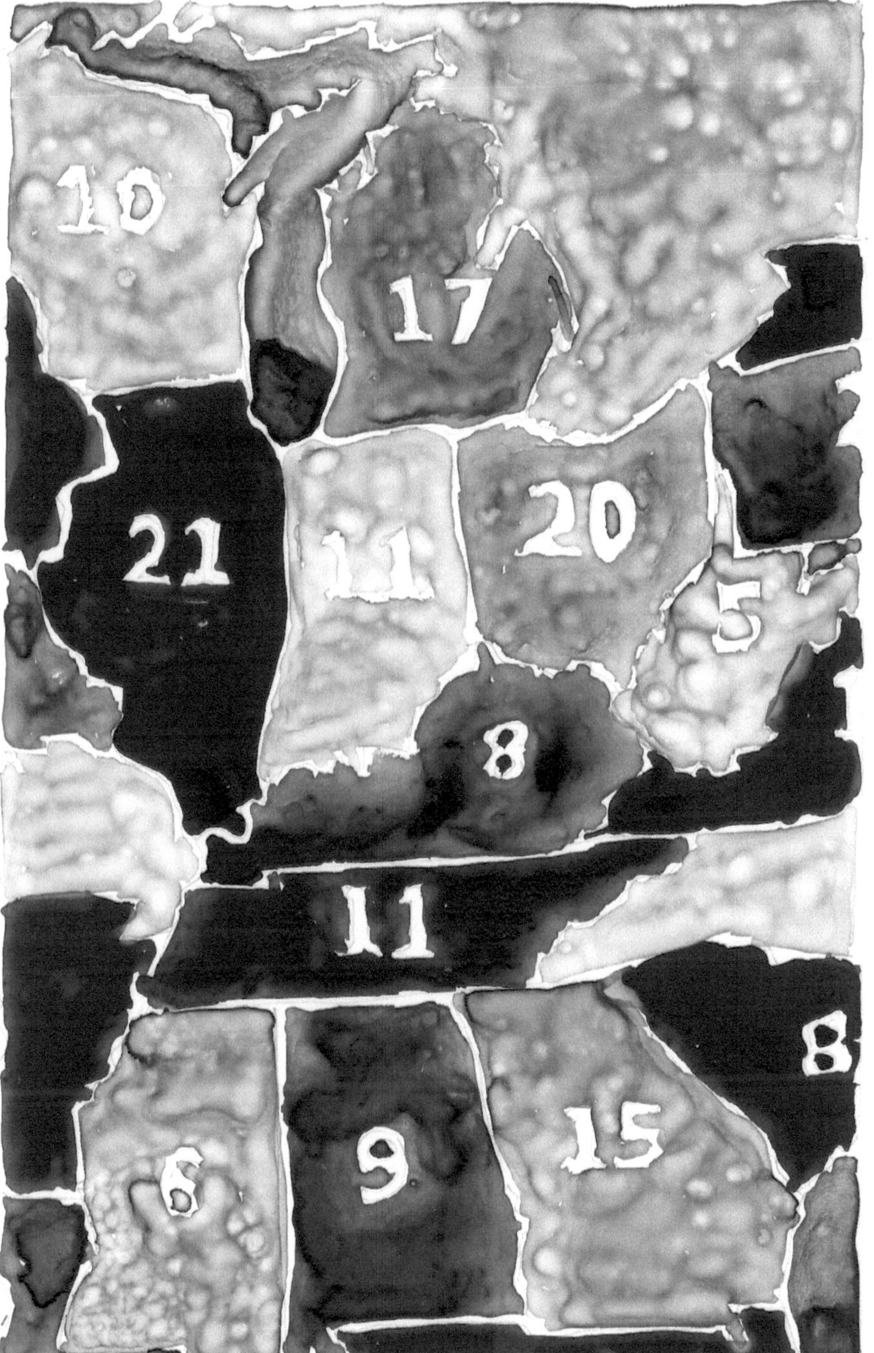
10
17
21
11
20
5
8
11
8
6
9
15

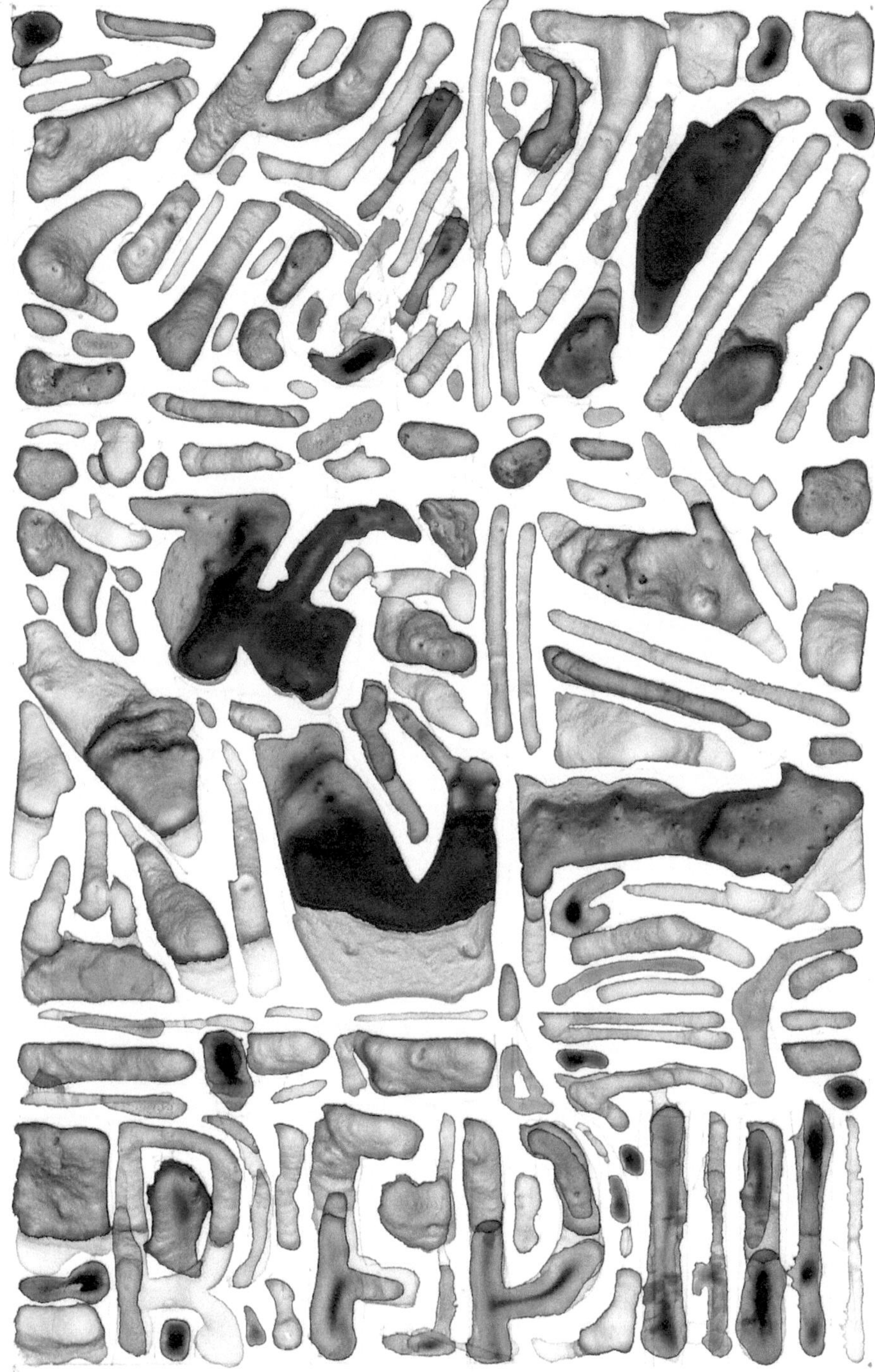

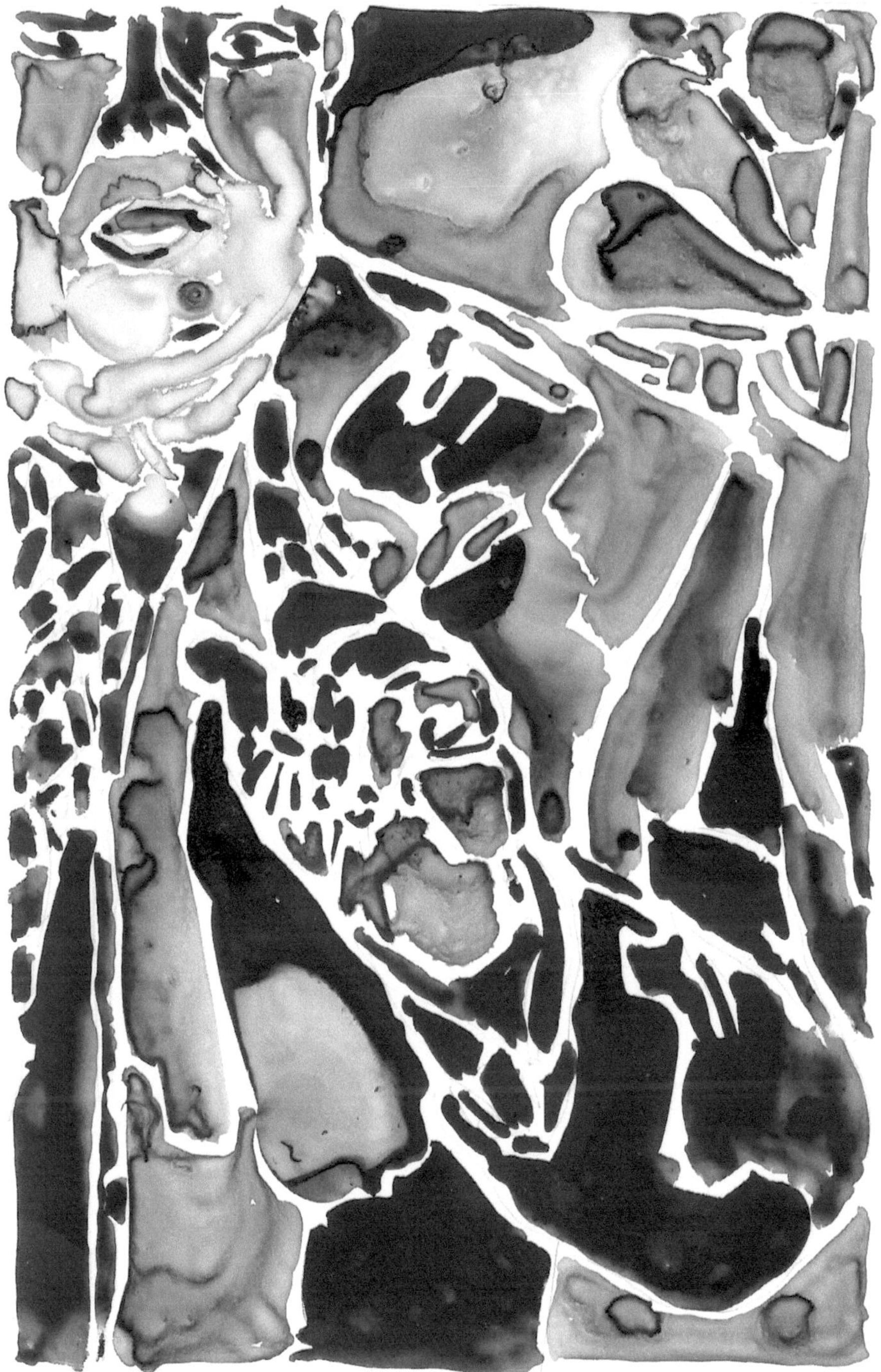

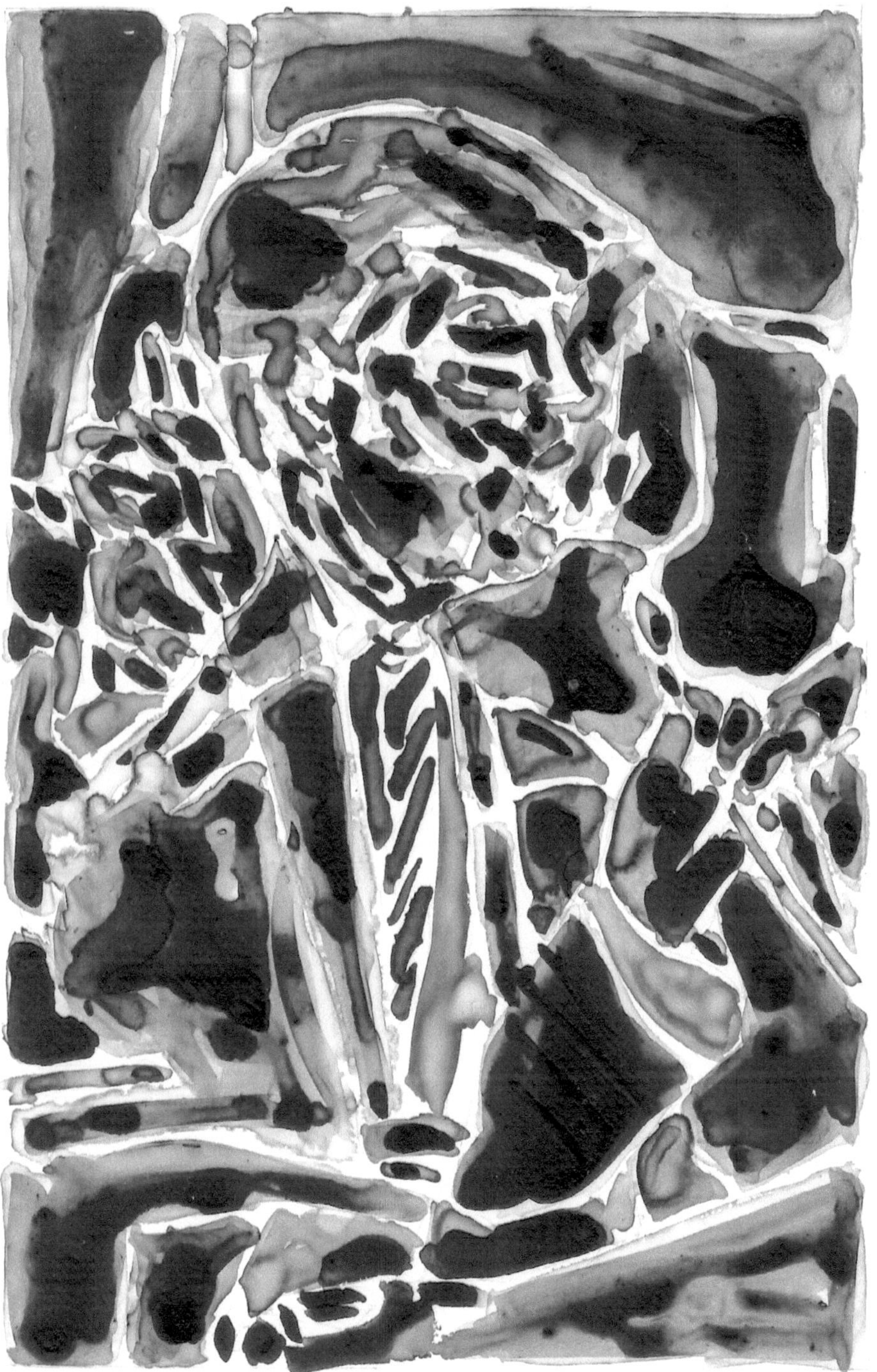

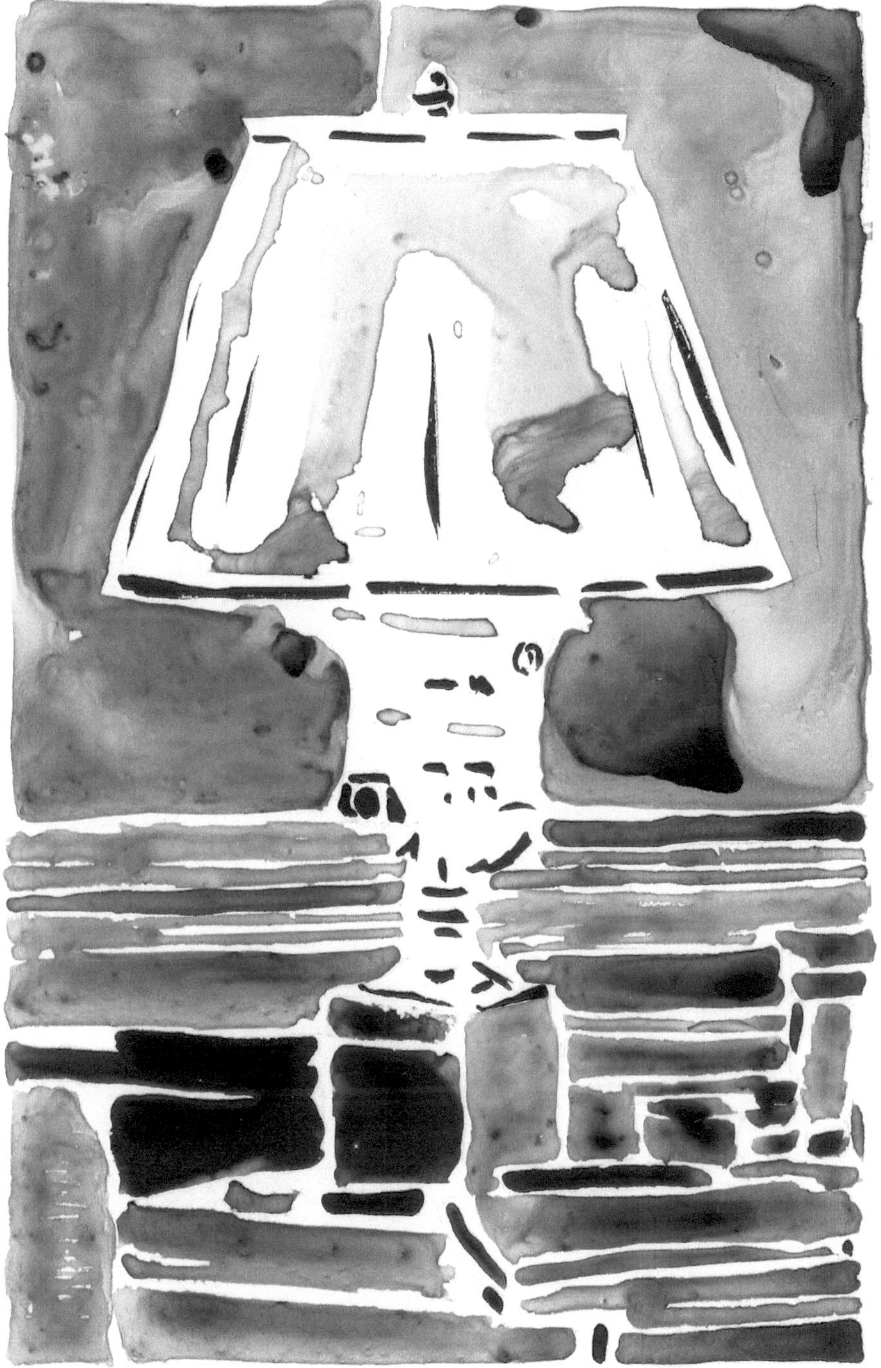

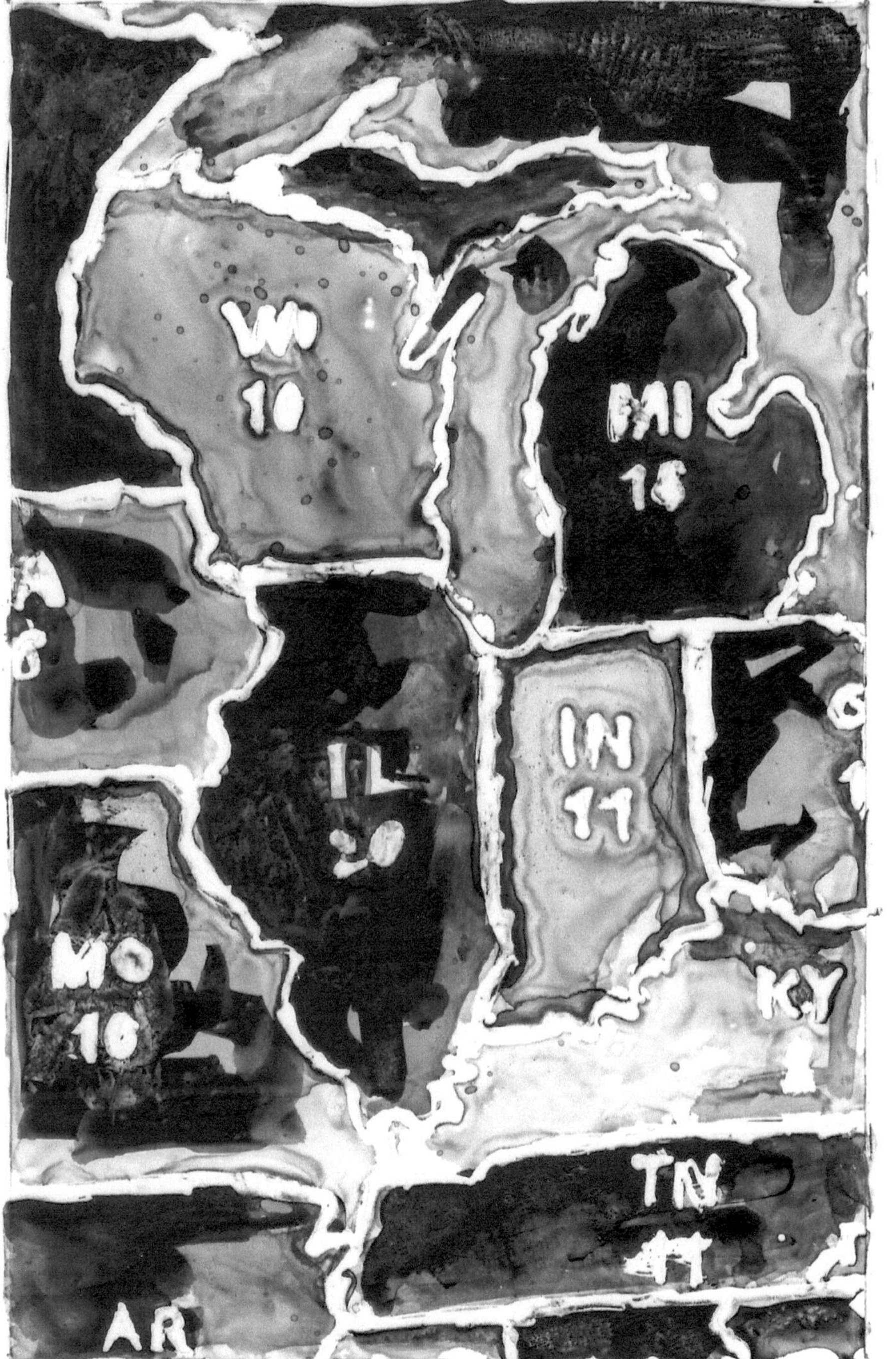
WI
10
MI
16
IL
IN
11
MO
10
KY
TN
11
AR

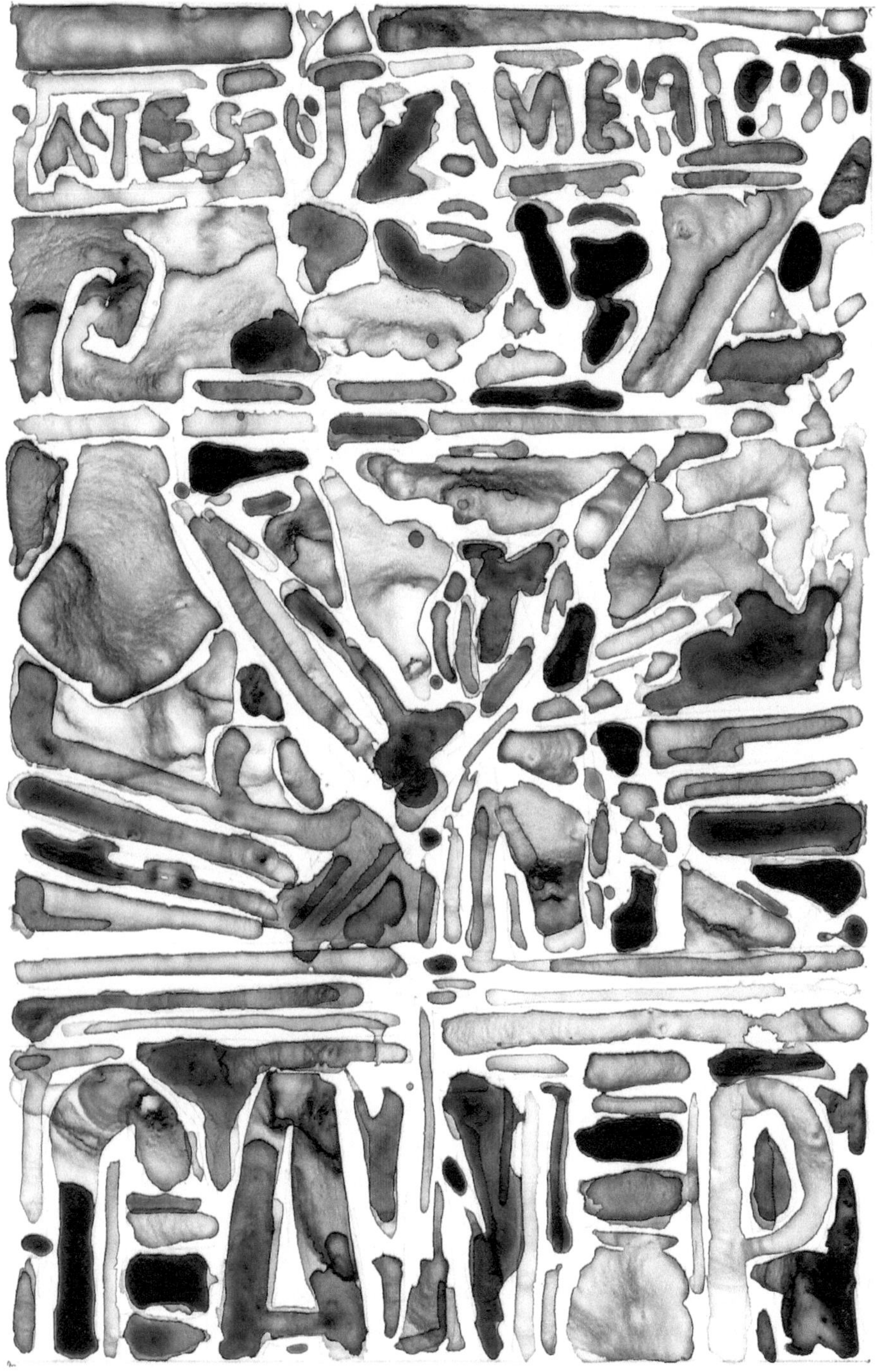

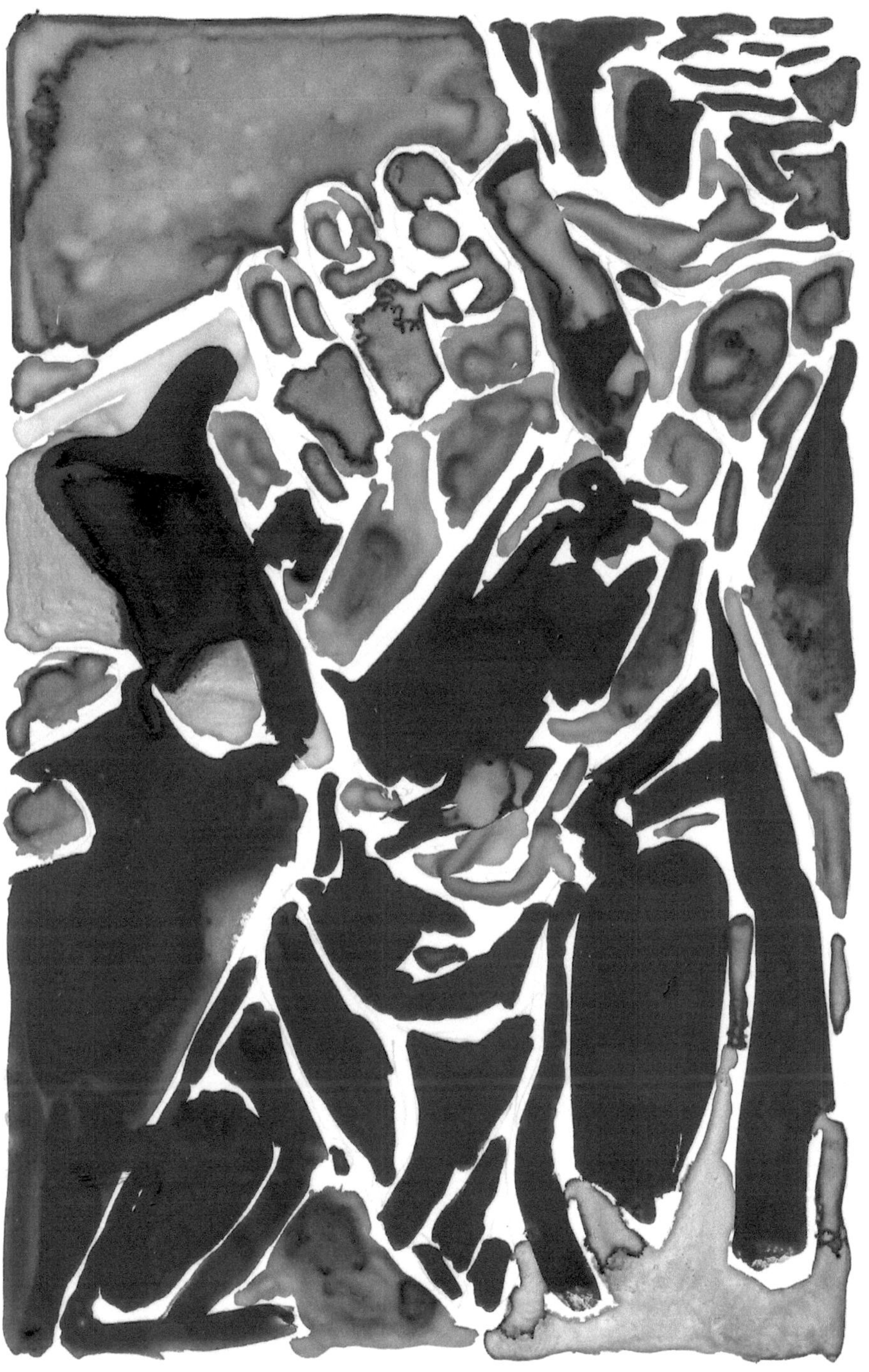

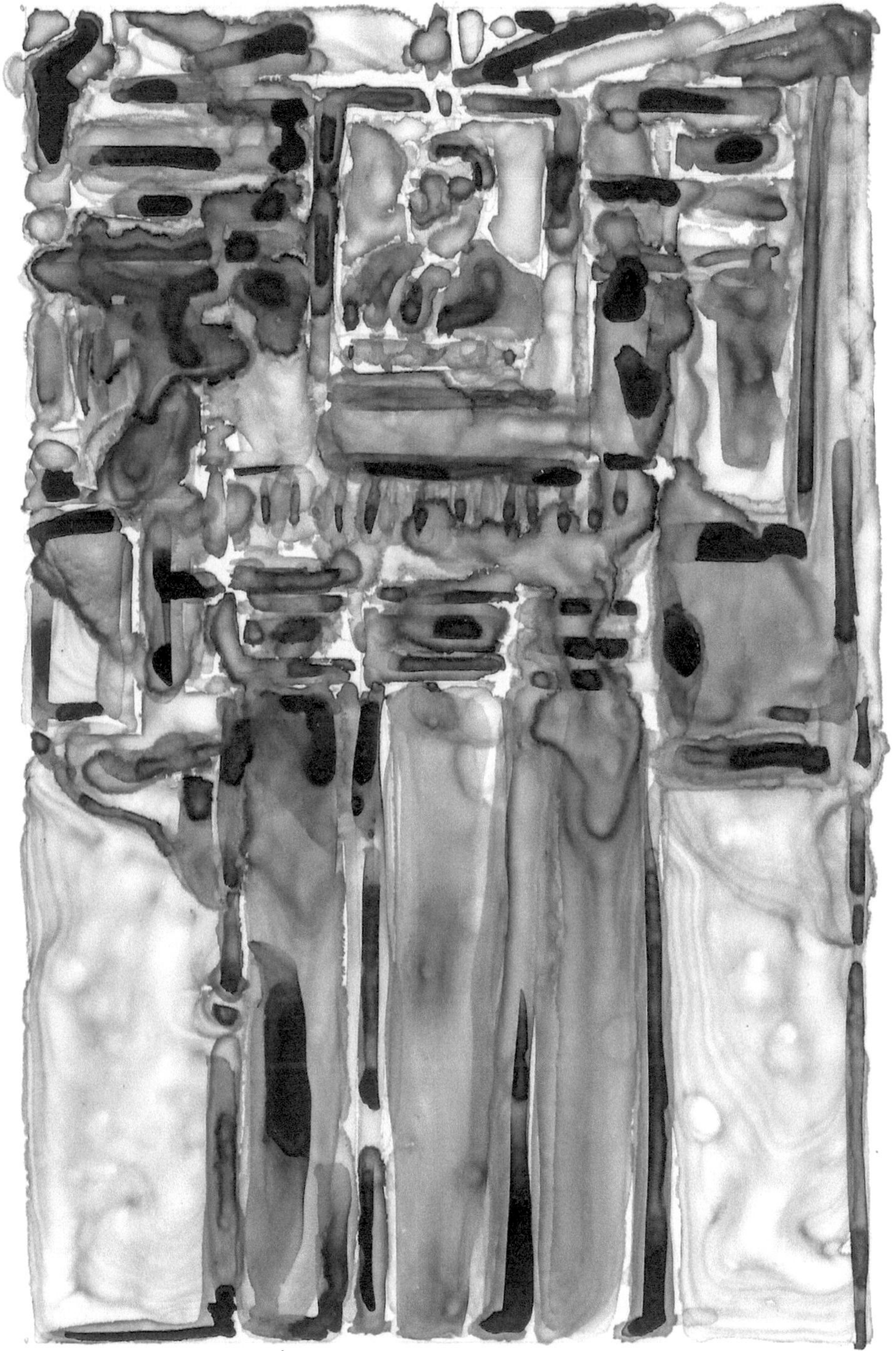

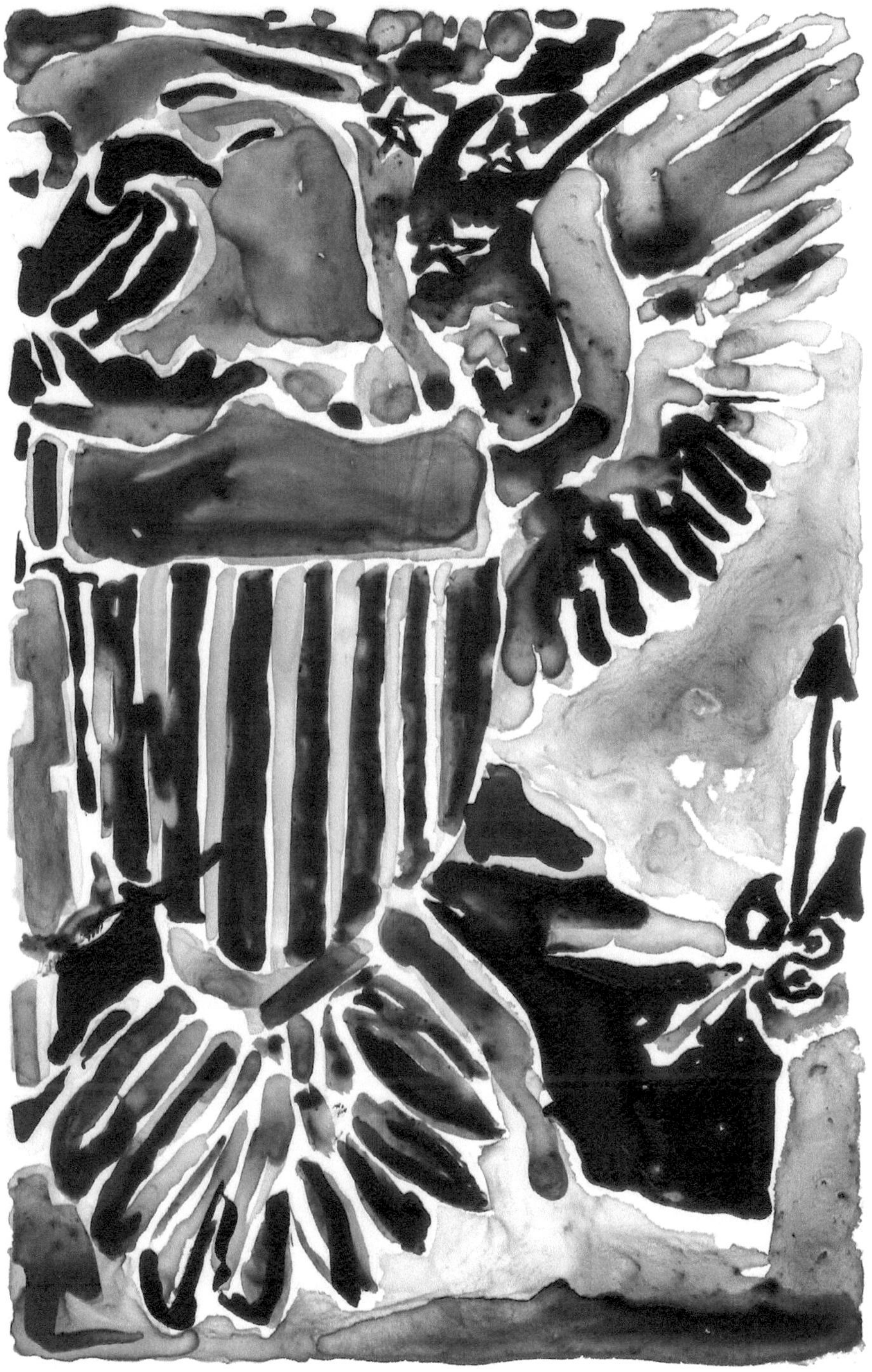

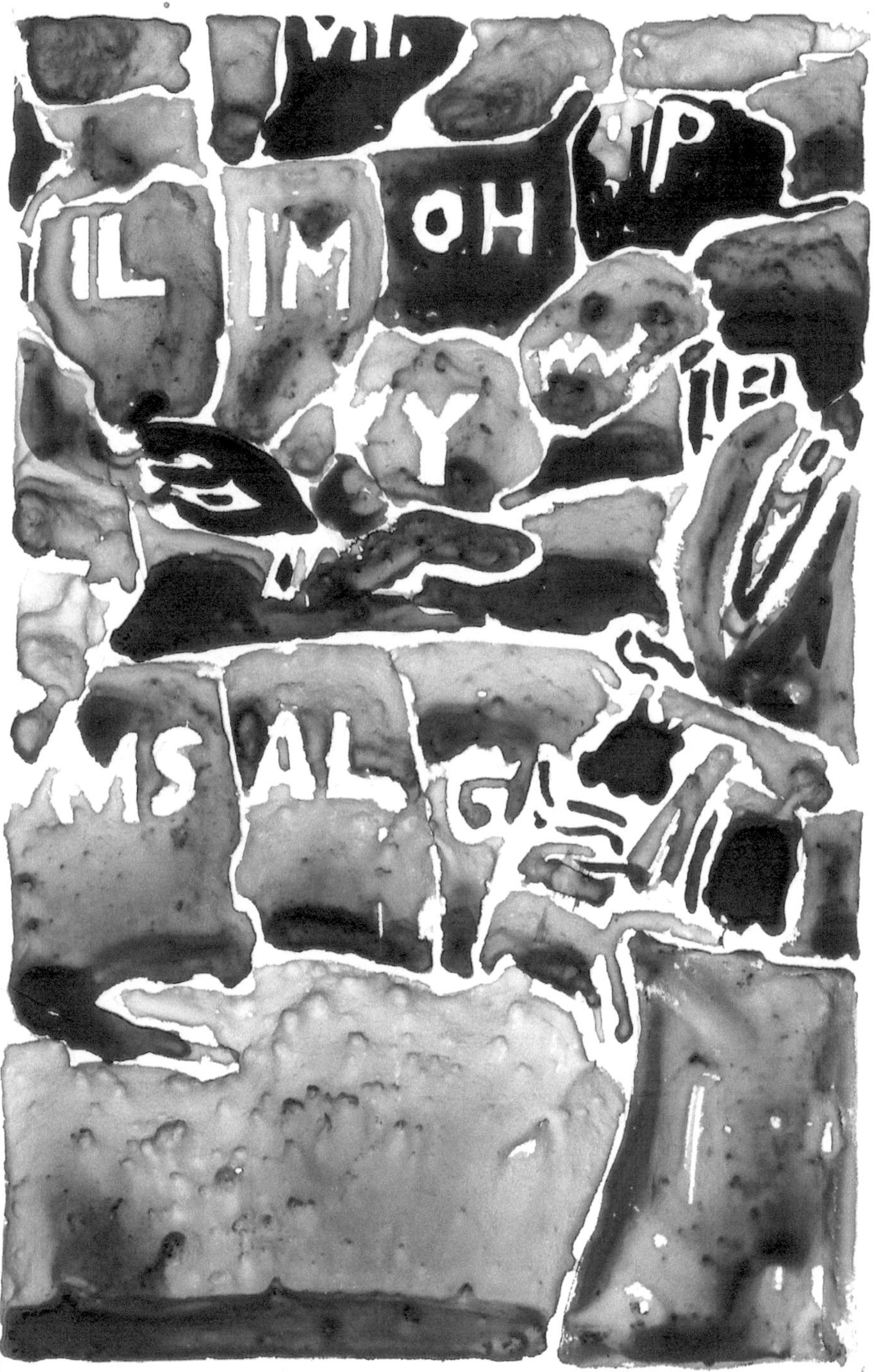
IL
IM
OH
UP
Y
MS
AL

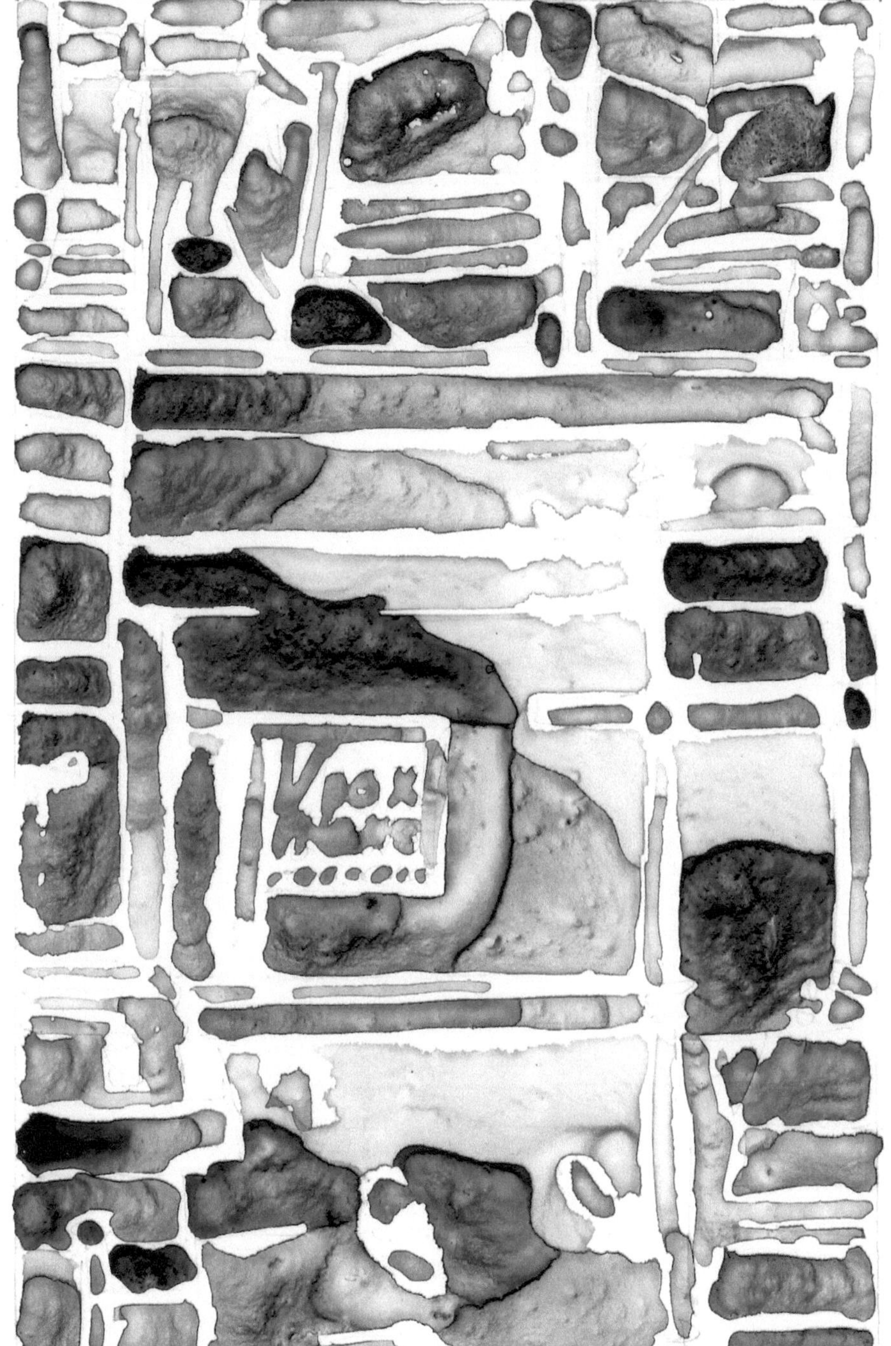

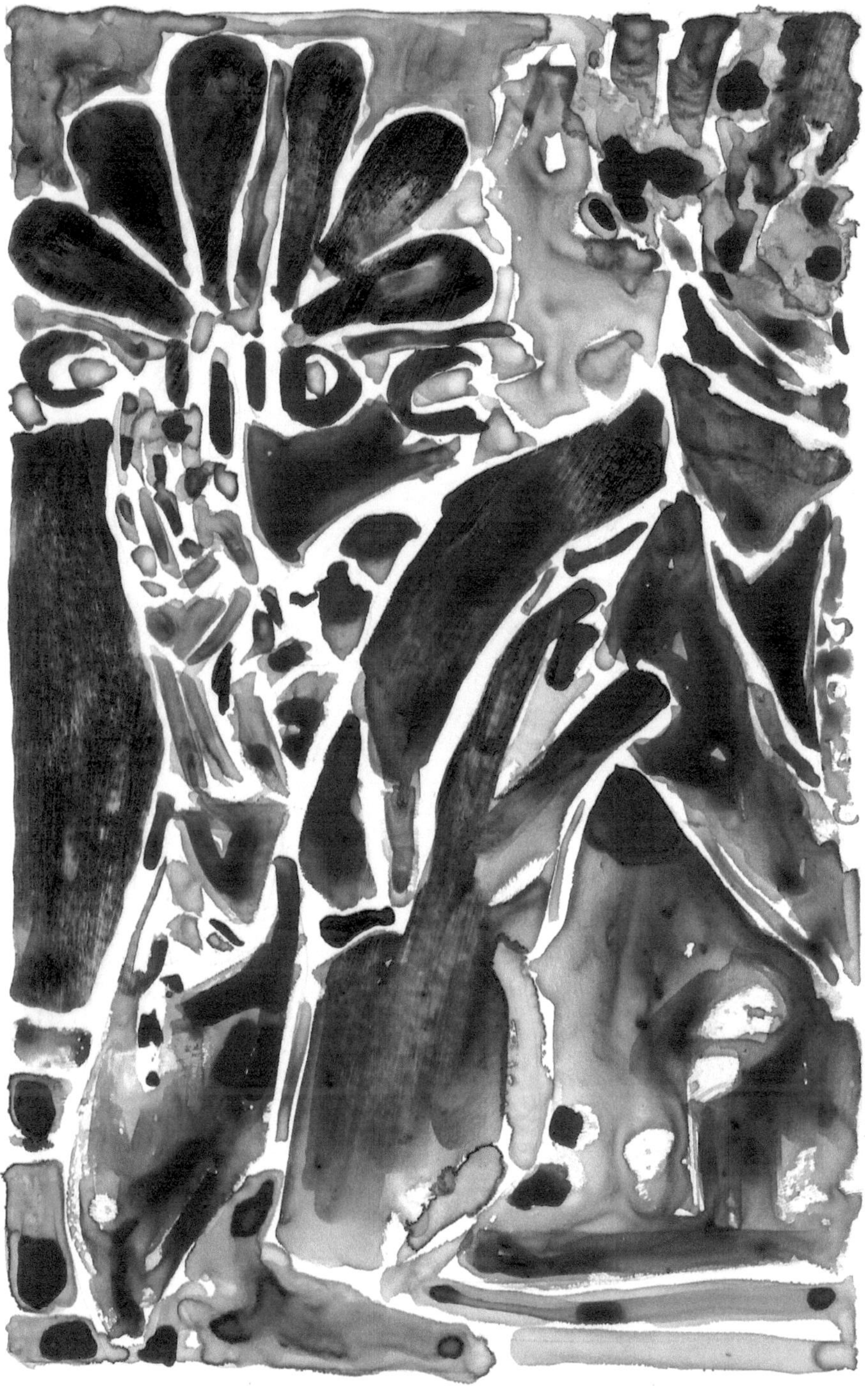

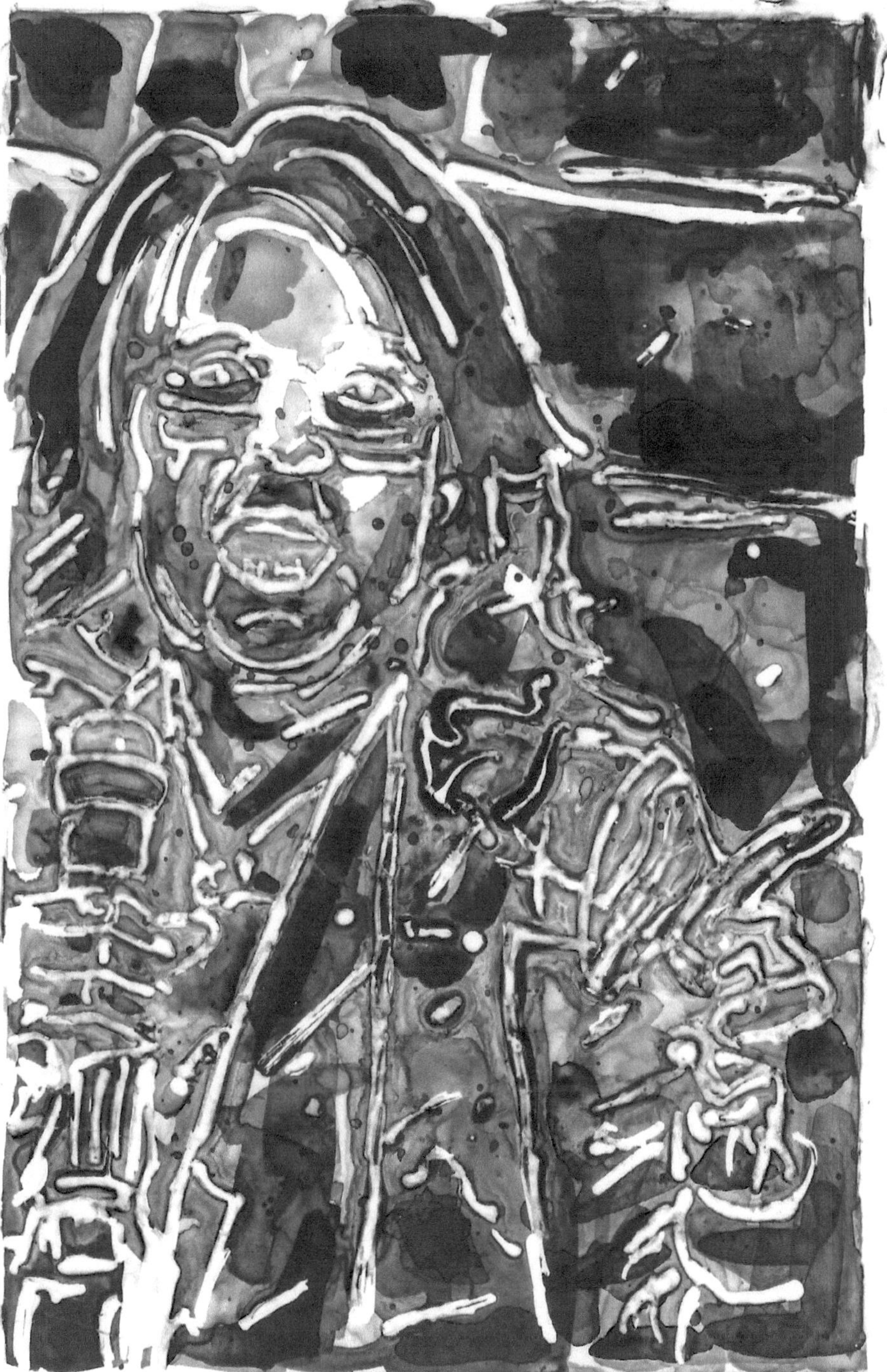

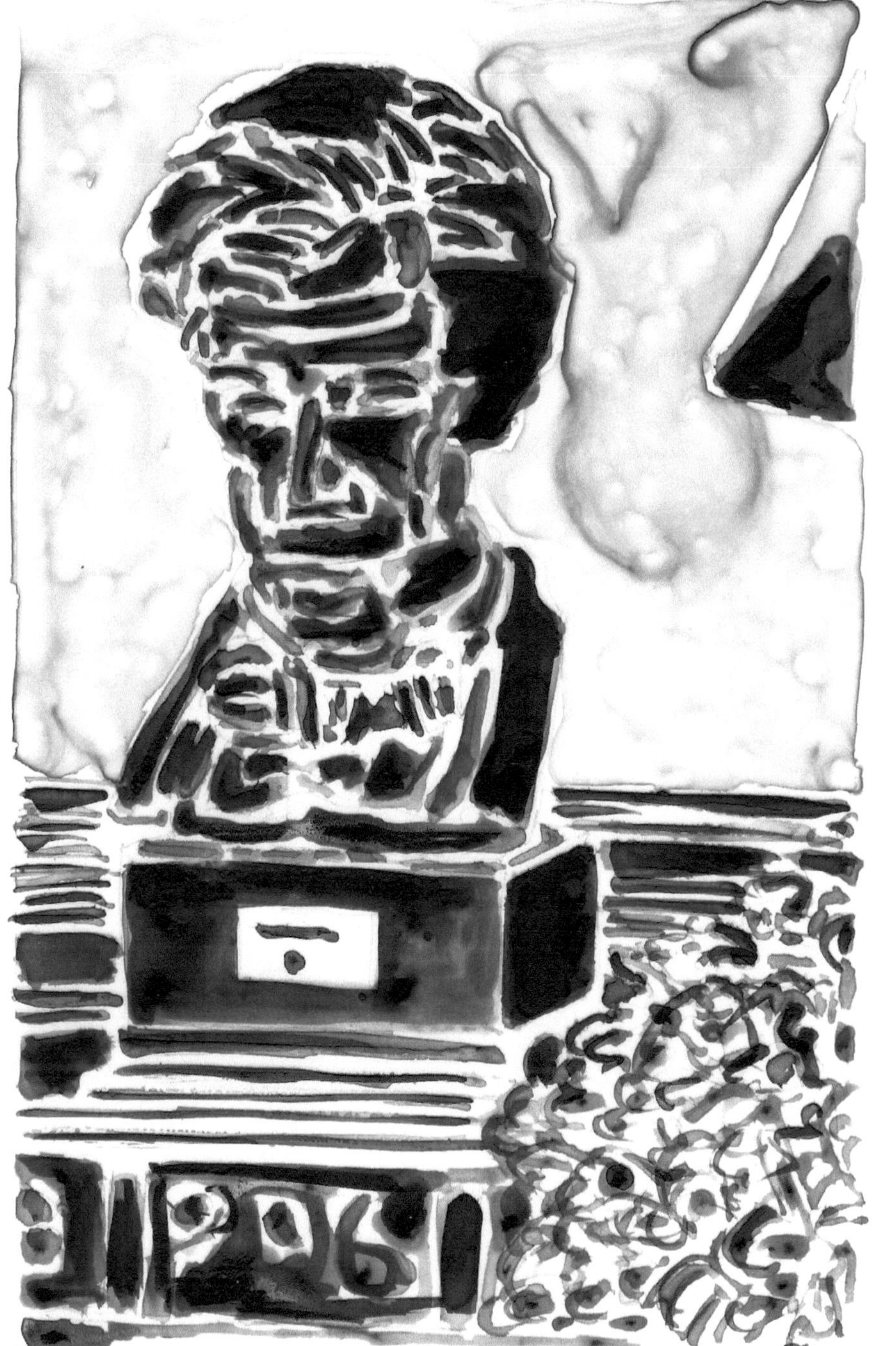
206

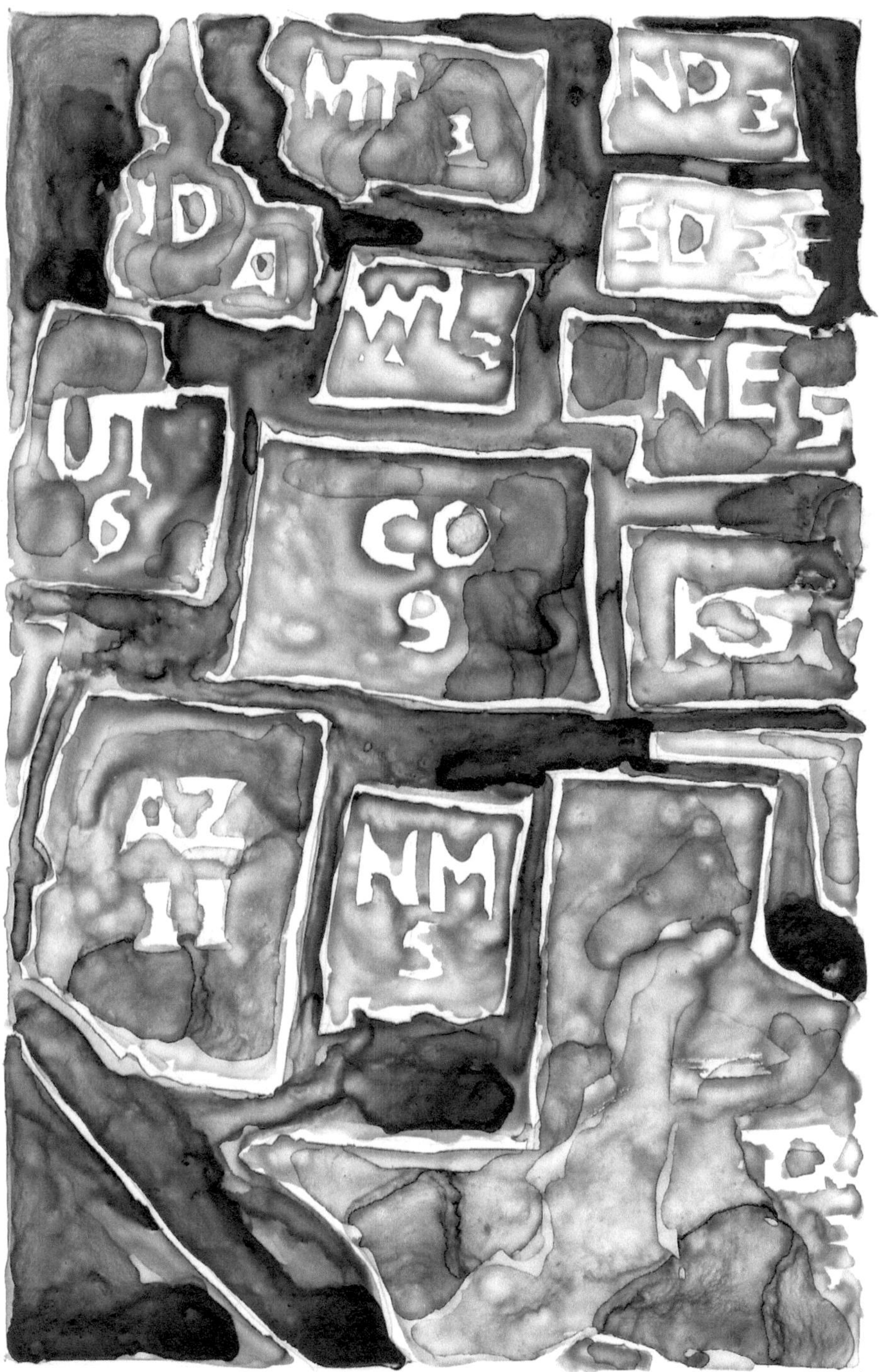
ND 3
UT 6
CO 9
AZ 11
NM 5

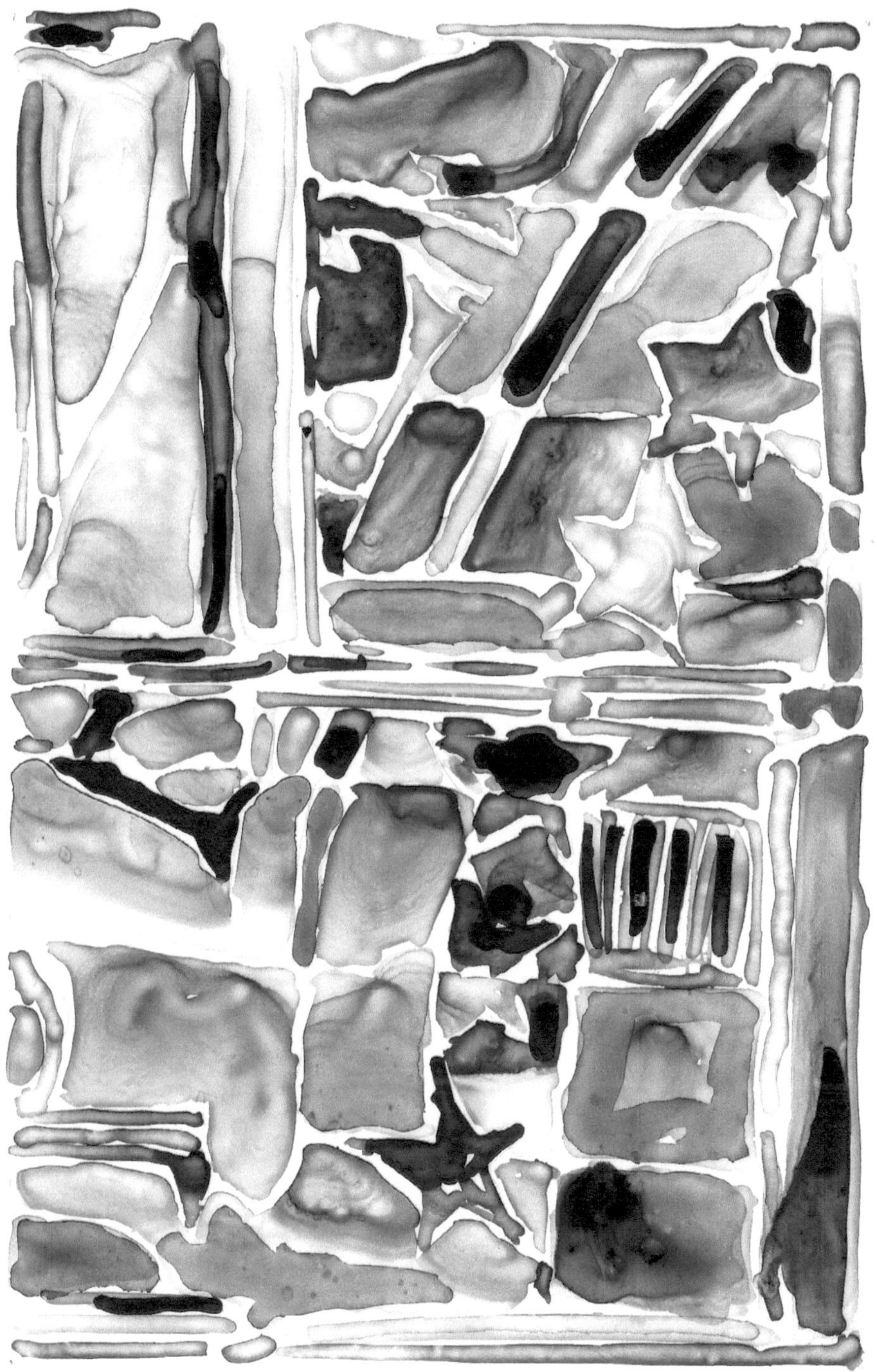

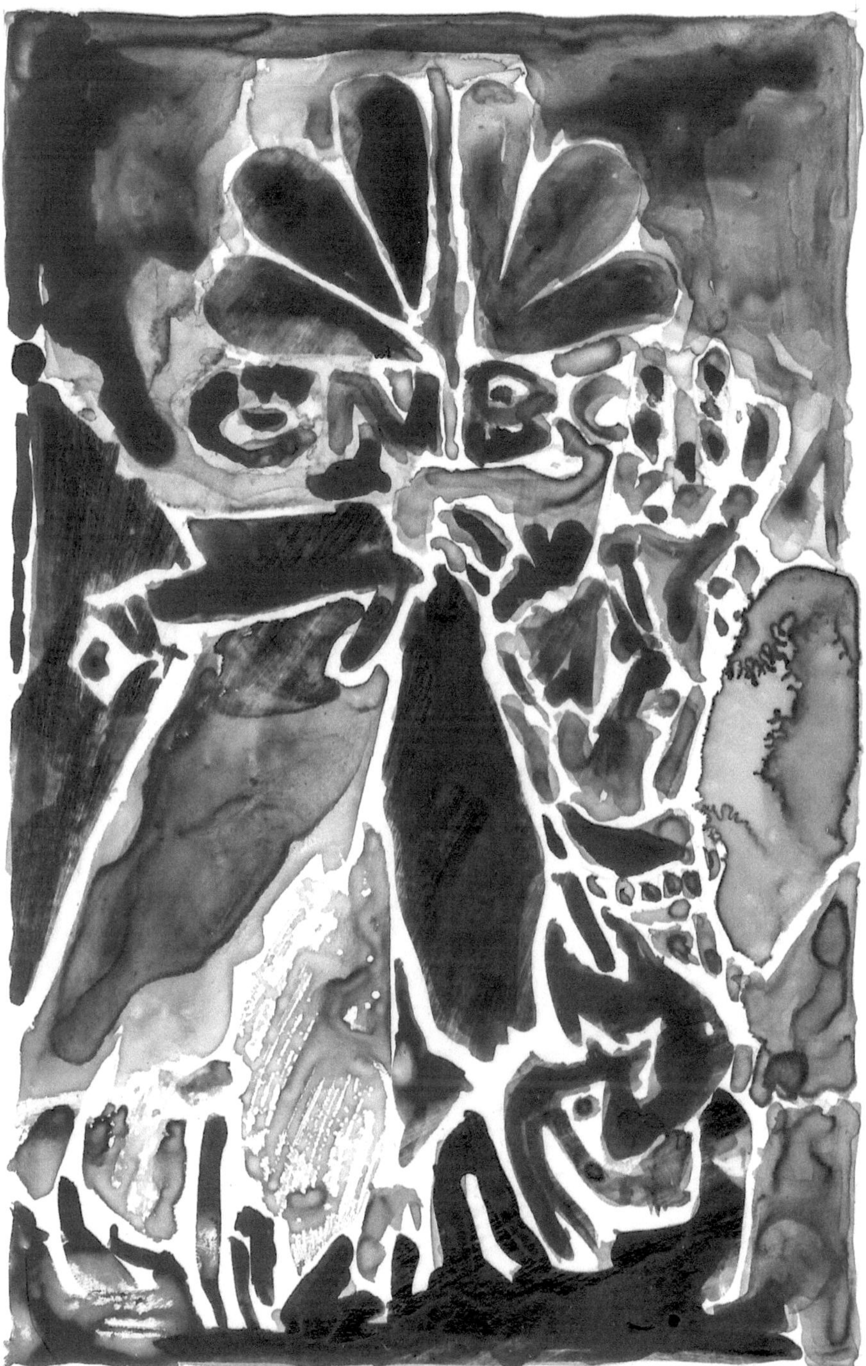

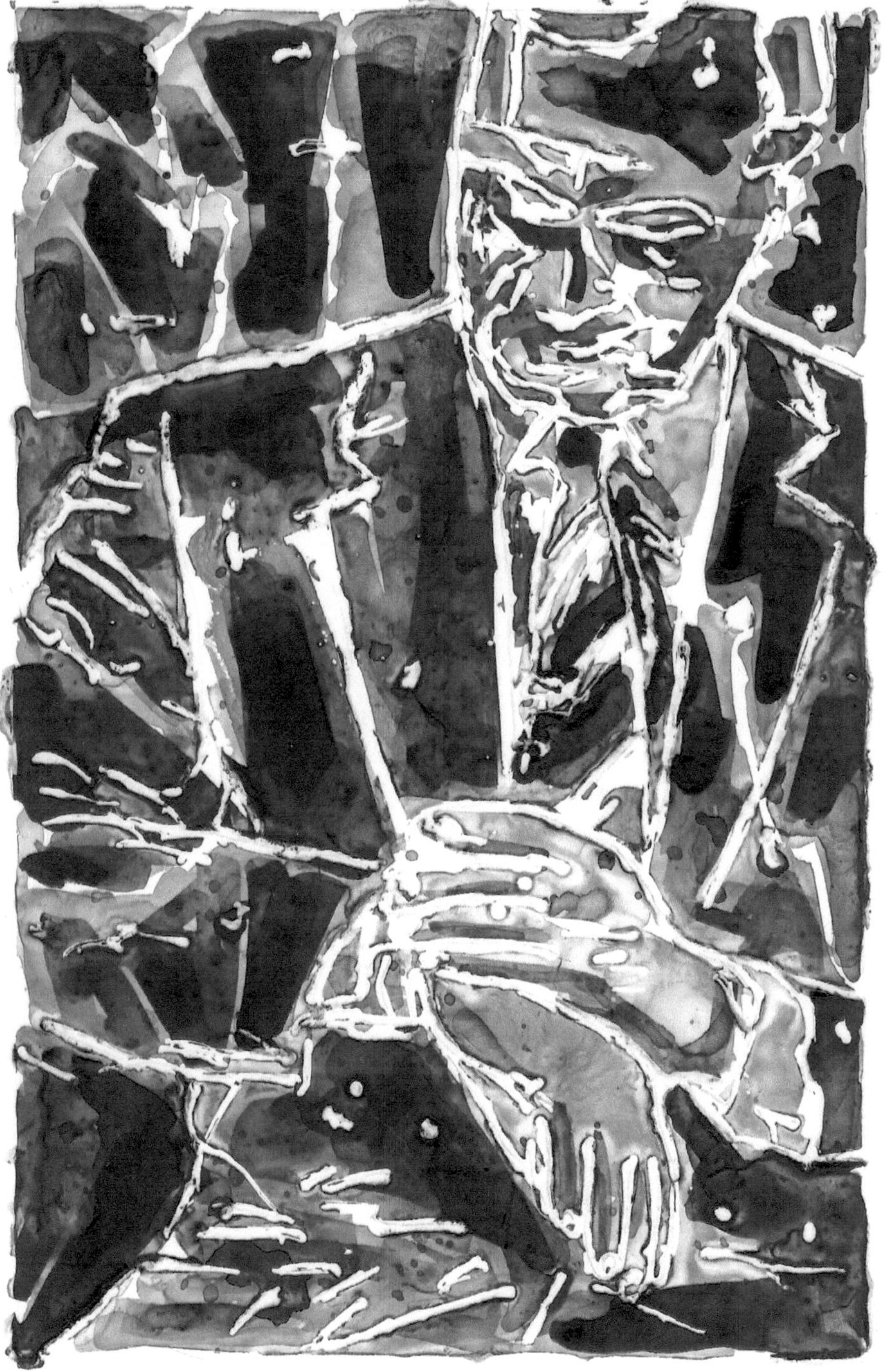

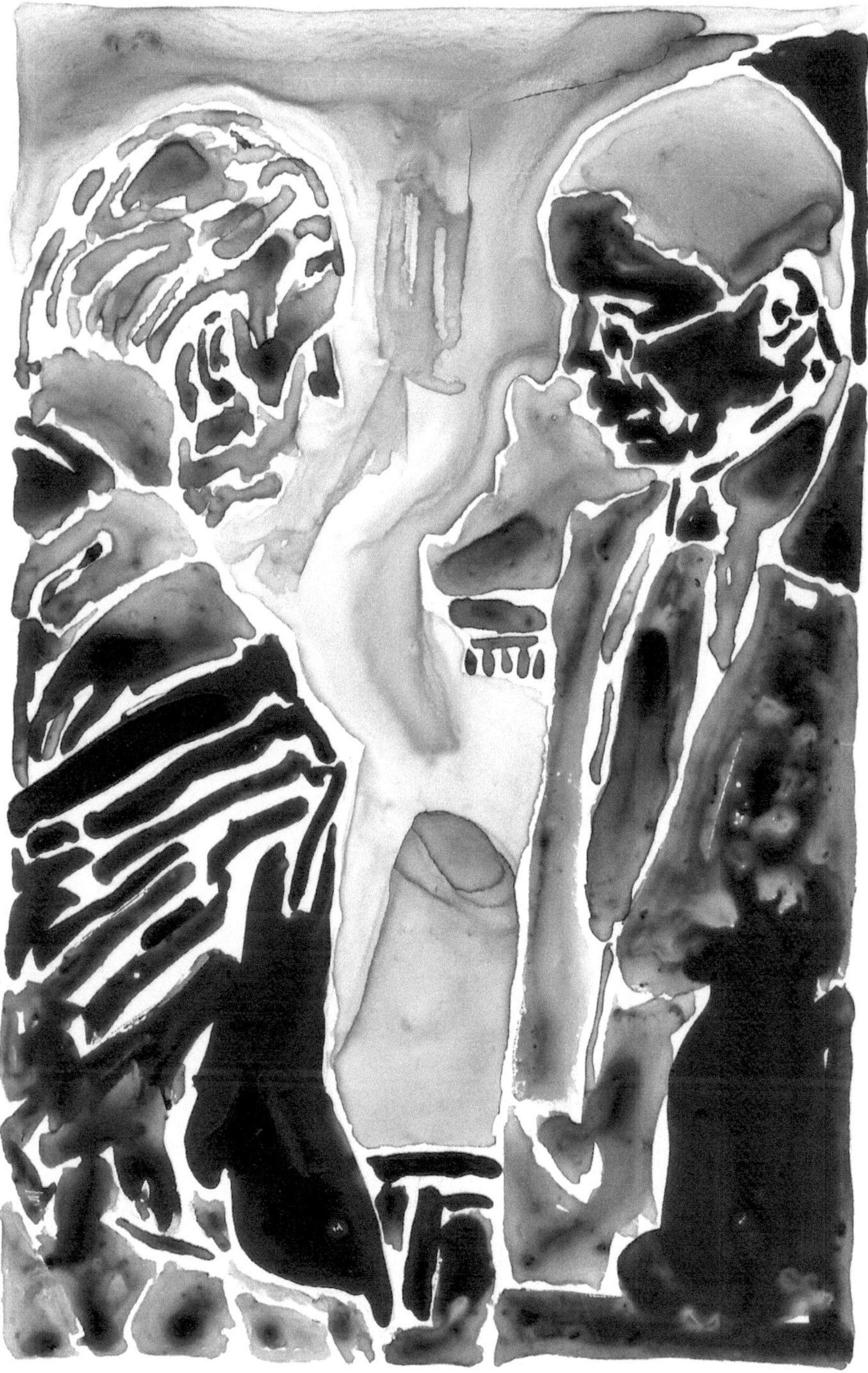

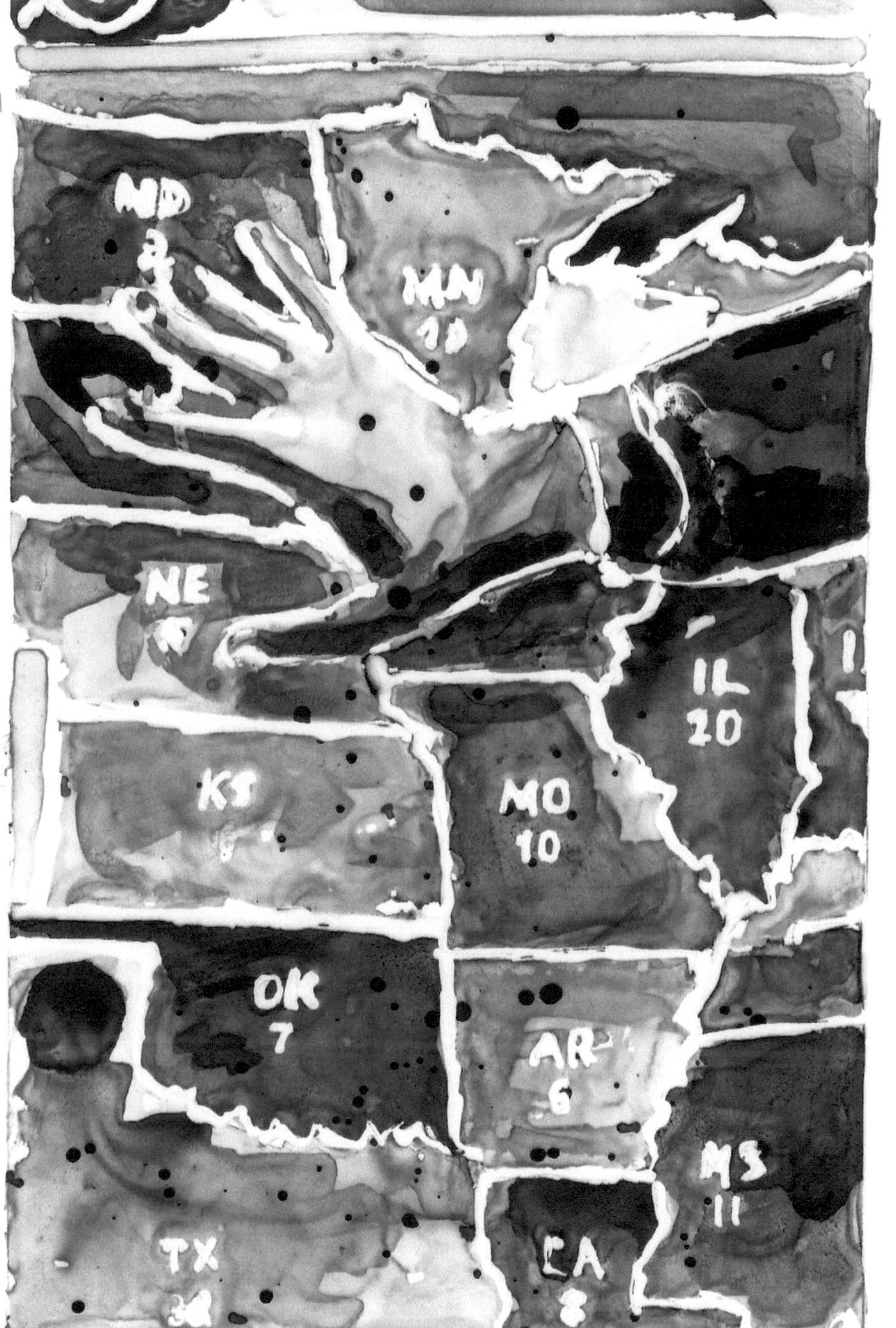
ND
MN
NE
KS
MO
10
IL
20
OK
7
AR
6
MS
11
TX
LA
8

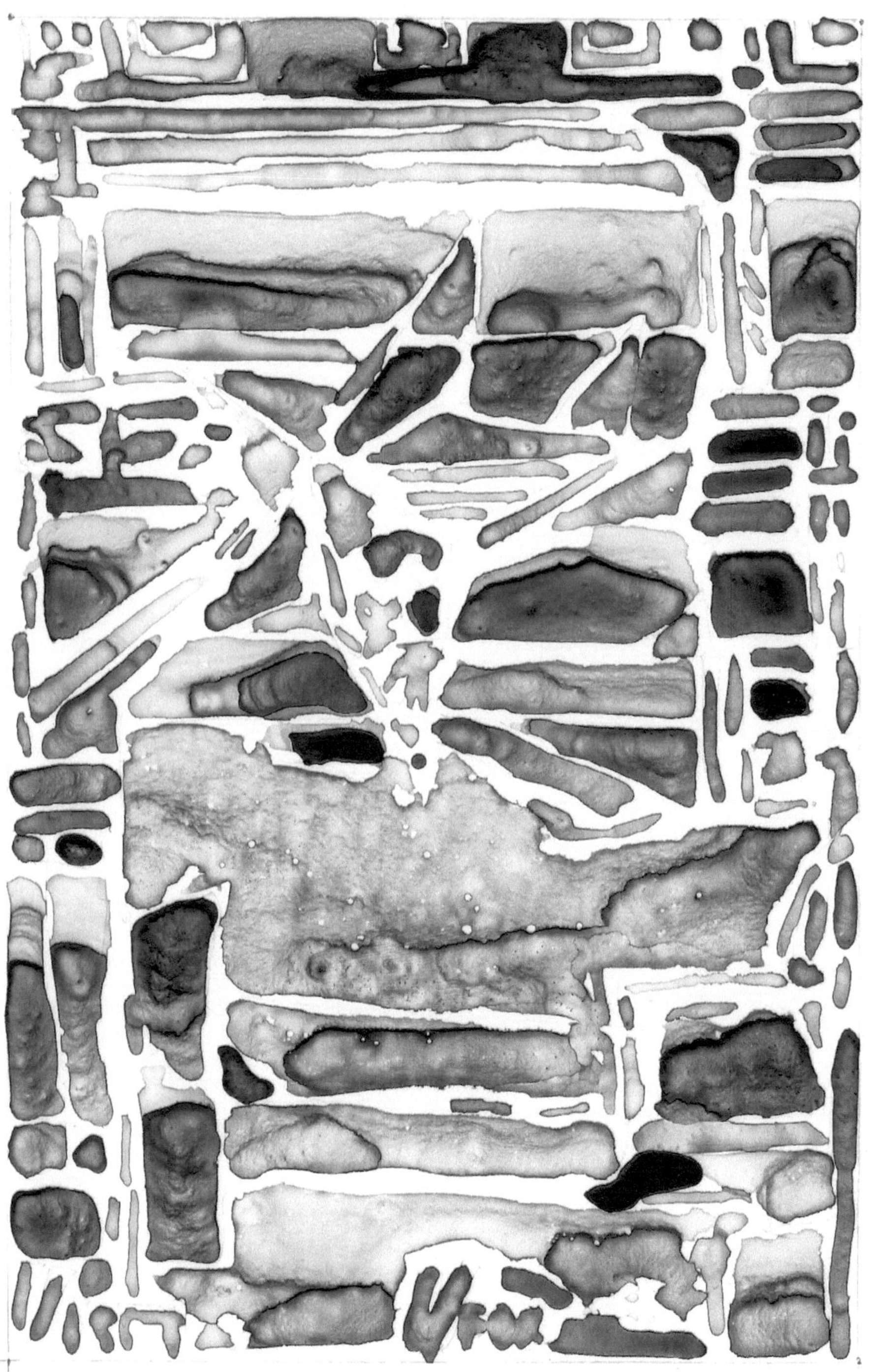

GUY BEN-ARI is a visual artist based in New York City. He is a current Artist-in-Residence at Triangle Arts Association and recently participated in the Keyholder Residency Program at the Lower East Side Printshop in New York. Guy is a SIP Award recipient from the Robert Blackburn Printmaking Workshop Program at The Elizabeth Foundation for the Arts, and a recent Artist-in-Residence at the Lower Manhattan Cultural Council's Workspace Program. Ben-Ari received his MFA from Columbia University's School of the Arts in 2011, and his BFA (with honors) from Bezalel Academy of Art and Design in Jerusalem in 2009, where he received the Presser Award for Excellence in Painting. In 2008, He studied Painting at the Slade School of Fine Art, UCL, London.

Ben-Ari's recent solo exhibitions were held at Scaramouche, NY, Vox Populi in Philadelphia, and Hamidrasha Gallery in Tel-Aviv. His work has been featured in exhibitions in New York City at Thierry Goldberg, Smack Mellon, Denny Gallery, The Jewish Museum, Fisher Landau Center for Art and SculptureCenter.

ERIC SUTPHIN is a writer and curator based in New York City. Eric received his BFA at Rutgers University and his MFA from the School of Visual Arts. Publications include; *Art in America*, *The Brooklyn Rail* and *Artcritical* in addition to exhibition catalogues and artist books. Curatorial projects include; *Rosemarie Beck: Paintings from the 60s* (New York, 2013) and *Detlef Aderhold: Signs* (Germany, 2015). Eric has been a visiting critic at Delaware College of Art and Design, The School of Visual Arts and Rutgers University.

www.ingramcontent.com/pod-product-compliance
Ingram Content Group UK Ltd.
Pitfield, Milton Keynes, MK11 3LW, UK
UKHW041936190726
13854UKWH00004B/1622